"Ours is a 110-year-old, fourth-generation family business. The authors of *Power Tools* played the key consulting role in our transition from third- to fourth-generation leadership and in our preparation for battle in today's volatile business environment. This book shares their surprisingly simple strategies and secrets, surely as applicable to your business as they were to ours." —Scot Hillman, General Manager, J. D. Heiskell & Co.; Past President, California Grain and Feed Association

"I consider their Power Tools to be nuclear-powered in the effect they can have on your life and your business." —Jay Conrad Levinson, author of *Guerrilla Marketing*

"Over the years our law firm has advised hundreds of family-owned businesses. The spectrum of potential legal, financial, business, and family problems is daunting. *Power Tools* encapsulates the most critical business activities into a customized plan. There would be much less litigation if every family business utilized these Power Tools."
—George Martin, Esq., organizer of the Bakersfield Business Conference

"As the nonfamily CEO of a family business, I believe the principles and practices contained in *Power Tools* are essential to long term success." —Barbara Griswold, Past International President, Executive Women International

"Every business owner should complete the Power Tools System at least once a year." —Lou Barbich, Past President, California Society of Certified Public Accountants

THE
FAMILY
BUSINESS:

POWER TOOLS
FOR SURVIVAL,
SUCCESS,
AND
SUCCESSION

ROGER C. ALLRED, C.P.A.,
AND RUSSELL S. ALLRED

BERKLEY BOOKS, NEW YORK

THE FAMILY BUSINESS:
POWER TOOLS FOR SURVIVAL, SUCCESS, AND SUCCESSION

A Berkley Book / published by arrangement with
the authors

PRINTING HISTORY
Berkley trade paperback edition / July 1997

The Putnam Berkley World Wide Web site address is
http://www.berkley.com

ISBN: 0-425-15773-3

BERKLEY®
Berkley Books are published by The Berkley Publishing Group,
200 Madison Avenue, New York, New York 10016.
BERKLEY and the "B" design
are trademarks belonging to Berkley Publishing Corporation.

PRINTED IN THE UNITED STATES OF AMERICA

10 9 8 7 6 5 4 3 2 1

To our mother and our wives for giving us life and making our lives worth living.

Acknowledgments

We wish to acknowledge our family business clients used as examples in this book, for their courage, faith, and for the privilege of working with them.

Our heartfelt thanks to Natalee Rosenstein and the entire staff at The Berkley Publishing Group for taking a chance on two first-time authors.

A thousand thanks to our agent, Michael Larsen. He and his partner, Elizabeth Pomada, motivated us to submit our best work and it worked.

Thanks also to Camille Williams for putting her husband and children on automatic pilot and editing our proposal. Also for teaching us the difference between an acronym and an acrostic.

Contents

Introduction
  Your Business Is *Your* Business!.....................................1

Chapter 1—Family:
  A Family Affair 9

Chapter 2—Marketing:
  To Make It, You Gotta Market....................................33

Chapter 3—Management:
  Who's the Boss? 71

Chapter 4—Accounting:
  Crunching the Numbers 101

Chapter 5—Protection:
  Keeping It All in the Family..................................... 125

Chapter 6—Production:
  Making More with Less.. 153

Chapter 7
  Creating the Plan of Attack 177

Appendix
  Power Tools, Listed in Order 181

Introduction
Your Business Is *Your* Business!

You have probably asked yourself, "What can I do to make my business more successful?" That is the reason you are reading this book. You are hoping that this book will give you the answers without the necessity of hiring an outsider to tell you what to do. Out siders are expensive. They ask a lot of questions, a lot of personal questions. And there is no guarantee that their expensive advice will be of any use.

With this book, you can protect the privacy of your business and still get the help you need. You can use the strategies or "Power Tools" of a top-quality consultant at a fraction of the cost. Consider the following two experiences from our consulting practice.

The Proud Patriarch

"I don't need a consultant telling me that I'm losing money," snorted the founder of a once thriving business. The truth was that he did need help. He just did not want anyone else telling him what to do. His position as the president of the family business was already under attack by family employees. Someone from the outside confirming his failings was more than he could handle.

The president had participated in the inception and growth of a multimillion-dollar operation that was now in bankruptcy. Family jealousy prevented him from accepting good advice from his brother, the vice president. Pride prevented him from seeking outside help. We performed a business evaluation as the Chapter 11 bankruptcy trustees. The solutions to the business's problems were found in the family members who were already involved. They were skilled in their industry and had a fine reputation. They just needed some help in creating an action plan and an opportunity to use their skills. They needed Power Tools, intellectual Power Tools. After the Power Tools were implemented, the company was sold to the younger generation and it now thrives.

We realize how hard it is to expose your business to outside scrutiny. In the process, the outsider might see something that you consider personal. We ask, Who's the best person to tell you that your zipper is down or that your slip is showing? Of course you would prefer that a family member catch you before you leave home. We developed the system in this book so you can prepare an action plan specifically tailored to your business without the aid of an outsider. You can maintain your privacy and still get the help you need.

The Phoenix

Greek mythology tells the legend of the phoenix, a bird that burns itself on a funeral pyre and then rises from its own ashes with renewed youth and beauty. Such was the case with this next example.

A forty-five-year-old, second-generation family business had lost over $1 million in one year. The owner contacted his attorney because the secured lenders were circling like buzzards over a corpse. The owner had personally guaranteed the secured debt and the creditors were demanding payment or they would seize his personal assets. Many unsecured creditors had successfully sued for payment and were attempting to execute their judgments. The owner was contemplating bankruptcy and was hoping to protect a small nest egg in order to live modestly for the rest of his life. The owner's attorney wisely recommended that the owner discuss the situation with us before taking any further action. The owner hired us, bankruptcy was avoided, equity was protected, and the business was not only saved, but *net income in the first year after implementing our Power Tools approximated $1.5 million.*

Power Tools are not magical but they were effective in helping turn this business around. This is what we did:

1. Performed a business evaluation to determine the attitudes of management, the real and perceived strengths and weaknesses of the business, and the financial status of the company.
2. Contacted and reassured the secured creditors that corrective action had begun. They were relieved to know that the right kind of assistance was being given to the company. They extended time to create a plan.
3. Held a strategic planning session with management to determine the options available, the vision and mission of the company, and to create a plan of attack.
4. Prepared a cash flow analysis and a proposed payment plan.
5. Negotiated with the secured lenders and finalized the payment plan with them.
6. Sold assets and downsized the business to free up cash and make the business more competitive in the current economy.
7. Identified a market niche where the company could earn a good profit margin and created a plan to abandon operations where the profit margin was slim or nonexistent.
8. Created a marketing plan to address the customers of the new, refocused, and streamlined company.

9.   Negotiated with other lenders to have a fallback position.
10. Negotiated with vendors for significant reductions in amounts owing for prompt payment from asset sales. These reductions included creditors with legal judgments.
11. Instituted a monthly management planning meeting to monitor progress and to respond to any variances from the plan.

This phoenix story can be replicated if all the right elements are in place. The whole process cost this owner around $10,000. Was it worth it? It was worth one hundred times that amount! Could they have done it without our help? Probably, if they followed the same sound business strategies that we guided them through.

As family business consultants, we see the same types of situations over and over again. Family problems and infighting undermine production. The next generation isn't prepared to assume control. Those in power won't relinquish control. Family members do not have the needed technical skills. Nonfamily managers are not trusted by some family members. These are signs of troubled companies. They need Power Tools.

Successful companies have troubles too. "We've hit a plateau." "How do we maintain control of this burgeoning business?" "How do we motivate nonfamily employees?" "How do we remain competitive in the current marketplace?" The solutions to these troubles may be found within the family but the family may need help seeing the solutions. They, too, need Power Tools.

We are brothers in a family-owned business. Roger is a CPA and business turnaround expert. Russ is a marketing consultant with a proven track record of increasing sales. As you read the book, you will notice that we often illustrate the Power Tools with personal exeriences. We have modified the stories to protect the identity of our clients.

Neither this book nor any other can be totally comprehensive. Using the Power Tools explained herein will not guarantee success, but each Power Tool that you implement will increase the odds that your business will be one of the few survivors.

How to Use This Book

The Family Business: Power Tools for Survival, Success, and Succession is not just a book. It is a system to evaluate and improve your business. These are the steps to implement the system:

Step 1 Make a copy of the Power Tools in the Appendix.

Step 2 Give your business a score for each Power Tool as you read the book.

Step 3 Create a prioritized action list.

Step 4 Implement each Power Tool from your prioritized action list.

Here is an example:

Item	Score	Weight	Power Tool
27	0	3	All understand that sales is their major function.
28	1	1	Management knows the customers.
29	0	2	Management has personal contact with large customers on a regular basis.
30	2	3	Management is dedicated to quality service and products.

The Item number indicates the order in which each Power Tool is explained in the book. Give your company one of the following scores in the Score box:

    0—Nothing being done or performing poorly
    1—Adequate performance
    2—Good or excellent performance
    N—Not applicable

Each Power Tool has a Weight which indicates its relative importance to the success of your company. The purpose of the Weight is to prioritize your action list:

    1—Important
    2—Very Important
    3—Critical

> *To make this system easier for you, we created Power Tools Action Plan Software. The software will prioritize your list for you and print a customized action plan. Refer to Chapter 7 for ordering information.*

The first six chapters explain the Power Tools that all companies should use. At the end of chapters 1 through 6 we have included a list of the Power Tools discussed in that chapter. Chapter 7 and the Appendix summarize how to implement the action plan.

Chapter 1 – A Family Affair
    Discusses family concerns within a business.

Chapter 2 – To Make It, You Gotta Market
    Emphasizes marketing strategies.

Chapter 3 – Who's the Boss?
    Outlines management tools to maintain control.

Chapter 4 – Crunching the Numbers
    Identifies good accounting practices.

Chapter 5 – Keeping It All in the Family
> Helps you protect your equity in the business.

Chapter 6 – Making More with Less
> Teaches techniques to increase production.

Chapter 7 – Creating the Plan of Attack
> Explains how to prioritize your action plan.

All businesses want to be successful, and success includes the survival of a business for many generations. You want your business to survive and grow so your grandchildren can benefit from the income. To create this legacy, you must implement sound business practices. Don't be discouraged if you feel that some of these Power Tools are beyond the skill level of your business as it currently exists. To develop a successful business you must have a vision of where the company is going. Prepare to be big by utilizing the Power Tools of a big business.

As you read the experiences presented in this book, you may think, How could anyone overlook that problem? or Surely that would never happen in my family. Try to be objective. One of the strengths of outside consultants is that they see things from a fresh perspective. They are not blinded by personal relationships. Look at your business as if you were evaluating someone else's.

You are now your own consultant.

1

Family: A Family Affair

Family Power Tools are those that are unique to a family business. They are typically ignored by business schools because "they are not business issues." These "non-issues" are what usually destroy successful family businesses and, sometimes, successful families.

Family businesses have emotional issues and they must be considered. Ignoring the passions that arise in a family business is like turning your back on a fire in your stockroom. You can ignore it for a while but it will eventually destroy your business.

Family businesses are also unique in that the family that owns the business has its own set of family values. These values can run the gamut from very strong to very weak. The truly successful family businesses have at least four essential values in common:

- Love or mutual respect that engenders a willingness to sacrifice personal wants for the benefit of the other family member(s).
- A dedication to maximizing the potential of individual family members.
- An understanding that integrity and family are more important than money.

- A desire to create a legacy that is worthy of being passed to the next family generation.

We have worked for many years with a family business in which these values are present. It is well into its second century of operation. The fourth generation has taken over from the third generation, and the young fifth generation is already being prepared for its turn in the driver's seat. The reason all generations have been successful in business is that they have taken care of the needs of the family in addition to the needs of the business. They have been true to their family values for generations. They have balanced love and money.

Since nearly two-thirds of all successful family businesses never reach a second generation, the following family Power Tools must be considered by any family business that expects to stay in business.

1. **The family business has the four essential plans for survival, success, and succession.**

Every family business needs these four plans:

1. The Family Plan: An overall plan of how the family benefits from the business. This plan is developed and modified through regular family business meetings.
2. The Strategic Plan: How the business will meet the financial objectives of the family and management. Family and non-family managers of the business must be involved in developing this plan. Strategic Plans must have tactical sub-plans in order for them to be effective. Tactical sub-plans define who is going to do what tasks and by when.
3. The Succession Plan: This is a plan that defines who is going to be the new boss and how that person is going to be prepared. The current owners will make this plan and then communicate it to the rest of the family.
4. The Estate Plan: This plan anticipates the death of the current owners and determines how the negative financial im-

pact of their passing will be mitigated. An attorney and tax accountant must be included in developing this plan.

2. The family has a mission statement for the business.

Most businesses today have identified a mission statement for themselves. A mission statement in its simplest terms is "Our business is successful because it provides our customers with . . . (fill in this statement)." Remember, however, that a mission statement is nothing more than a bunch of pretty sounding words if it isn't used as a standard by which all significant business decisions are measured. And in order for it to be used as a standard, the management team must all believe in it and support it.

A mission statement should not be vague. It loses its impact, however, if it becomes so lengthy that no one reads it. A properly crafted mission statement can appropriately be emblazoned over the door to the company headquarters. For example, our mission statement is "The mission of Allred & Associates, Inc. is to help our clients honorably achieve their objectives." It's short and sweet, and it reminds us of why our clients keep paying us.

3. The family has a vision statement for the business.

Although mission statements seem to be fairly common, vision statements are not. A vision statement is important for every business but essential for a family business. Your vision statement should state what you want your business to become. A vision statement is not customer-focused but rather ownership/family-focused. "Our business exists because it helps *our family* to . . . (fill in this statement)."

A vision statement must incorporate all that is important to the family in relation to the business. Family values will have a significant impact on what is included in the vision statement. Since this statement will be used to evaluate business decisions that affect how the business benefits the family, it is essential that it be developed by the family. Every attempt should be made to achieve consensus on the vision statement by all family members who have an interest in the business.

The following is an example of a vision statement from one of our clients: "Our vision is to be the most profitable company in the industry and a fun place to work."

4. Family values and objectives are incorporated into the strategic plan of the business.

Strategic plans are critical to the success of almost all organizations, family businesses included. A strategic plan should be developed by the business management team every year. The strategic plan must include the business mission, its vision, an analysis of the company's strengths and weaknesses along with company goals, and an action plan that details what needs to be done, by when, and by whom. Typically, the mission and vision of the company do not change significantly from year to year but the action plan will change dramatically.

In a family business, the strategic plan must take the family objectives into consideration. The strategic plan must also be in conformity with the family values. For example, if the family believes that family members and employees should not work on Sunday, the management team should not try to increase output by scheduling Sunday work.

5. Management knows the objectives of the family.

Families usually have certain expectations from the business. Conflicts arise when the family's expectations are not effectively communicated to the management of the company. It is impossible to reach a goal that has never been set.

This problem is certainly not limited to nonfamily managers.

Even very close family members who manage the business can be totally oblivious to what the other family members want from the business. Some family members might want immediate cash, others a stable, long-term income stream, and others just the pride of being recognized as a big shot in the community.

The first step is to determine the family's expectations and objectives. This is not always an easy task. In fact, it is almost impossible to accomplish unless the family has annual family business meetings to discuss the mission and vision of the business.

The second step is to communicate those objectives to management in a clear and concise way. Whining about what is not happening is not the way to communicate objectives. The objectives of the family must be in writing and should be discussed with the manager of the business on a regular basis so misunderstandings can be kept to a minimum.

6. Family business meetings are held regularly.

If every day is business as usual, there is no forum to resolve family issues and conflicts. Left unresolved, family issues and conflicts become business issues and conflicts. Family business meetings will deal with business issues. More importantly, they must deal with those topics that will affect whether or not the business can continue as a family business. This is the time and place to talk about topics that are too sensitive or personal to be discussed in front of nonfamily employees.

The family business meeting has to integrate the business needs and the family values. No business decisions can be made that conflict with the family values if the business is to survive. Family businesses, unlike most other businesses, have an identity that cannot be separated from the identity of the family itself. Any variance from the family values by the business will usually create a strong negative reaction from family members, which can cause them to replace management, leave the business, or create conflicts that will eventually destroy the business.

Family business meetings should be scheduled on a regular basis. The frequency of these meetings will depend on the needs of the business and the needs of the family, but a meeting must be held at least annually. Sometimes it is helpful to have a trusted nonfamily facilitator conduct such a meeting in order to keep the conversation focused on critical issues and away from petty ones.

7. Family members are competent in their assignments.

Thousands of businesses have failed because one member of the family relied on the ability of another member of the family who was incompetent to perform the task assigned to him or her. It does not matter if the task is production, marketing, management, or accounting. Businesses fail because of incompetence in any of these areas.

Many businesses have family members "handle the numbers" for fear of having an outsider know how well or how poorly the business is doing. Other businesses assign marketing duties to family members because "Anyone can buy advertisements." Still others assign the eldest son to be president of the family business because of tradition. These choices often lead to tragedy.

One company owner hired his daughter as the bookkeeper. He was paying her $8,000 a month to do the books. She had no formal training in accounting, had never worked as an accountant, and was not capable of creating an accurate financial statement. When we asked her what her responsibilities were, she said most of her time was spent monitoring the legal pleadings filed by the attorneys in the company's bankruptcy case. Is it any wonder they were in bankruptcy?

Gender, age, or family relationship should not determine suitability for any field of endeavor. It is satisfying to be able to offer a job to a loved one, but if that loved one is not capable of doing the assigned task, the result will be disastrous for the business and usually for the relationship.

8. Family members are compensated according to their contribution to the business.

All employees want to be paid for what they do. However, when family members are paid for who they *are* rather than for what they *do,* both morale and productivity problems arise. Other employees often become resentful. This resentment can lead to other problems that will affect coworkers, customers, and even other family members. Overpaid family members can get the impression that it really does not matter how productive they are. This impression can be a cancer that destroys not only the business but the moral character of the individual.

Family problems can also be created by undeserved compensation. Sibling or other family rivalry can be aggravated or even created by not compensating family members based on productivity. Overcompensating family members is almost always detrimental to the business and the family.

Sometimes family members are undercompensated for their efforts as a result of a belief by the founder that the family members should have to sacrifice for the benefit of the company. When family members are overcompensated, they usually stay with the company. When they are undercompensated, they are more likely to leave—mad!

9. Performance standards are the same for family and nonfamily employees.

Performance standards must be the same for all employees, regardless of familial relationship, if the company intends to maximize its potential. No one likes to work for a company that shows undeserved favoritism to certain employees. People often expect it from family businesses and they usually aren't disappointed! This tends to create higher turnover and a lack of trust in management.

Conversely, sometimes the family expects much more from family members because they are related. This can be just as debilitating as undeserved favoritism, because the family member feels as if he or she is being taken advantage of by the family. It also has a tendency to give family members the impression that the business is more important than family or anything else.

The only way to maximize the potential of the company and the individual family members is to establish fair expectations of employees and then treat everyone equally. There will be family members who will outperform the expectations because they realize it will be for their benefit in the long run, and they will not feel resentful about it.

10. Family disputes are handled in a predetermined manner so as not to inhibit operations.

Our Dad used to say, "You can't offend me, I'm too ignorant." If only it were true for all of us. All businesses have disputes just as all families have disputes. Therefore, it would follow that all family businesses have the potential for a lot of disputes. Hopefully the disputes are relatively minor, but there must be a way of resolving them in a timely, productive manner. No one likes to work in a business where work is impeded by what happened at the family Christmas party.

Russ met a young man, fumbling on crutches, at a function where Russ was speaking. He asked the young man if he enjoyed his skiing trip. The young man confided that his broken leg was the result of a disagreement with the company president, who happened to be his brother. We're sure when their father made his oldest son the president, he never intended for this to happen. They should have established a better method of problem resolution than "Take it outside, boys."

The method of handling family disputes might be to deal with them at family meetings, but sometimes that is just not soon enough. Probably the best way to resolve family problems is to deal with them just as you would any other business problem. This is easier said than done because most family disputes include an element of emotion unique to the family. The important thing to remember is that disputes must be dealt with quickly so as not to damage the operations of the company. When disputes cannot be resolved by the family in a businesslike manner, the family should select a mediator to assist them.

11. Children who will work in the family business start working in the business at a young age.

Teaching a healthy work ethic is one of the most important things that a parent can do for a child. Owners of a family business have a unique opportunity to do so by giving the child a job in the business. We know a man who was a cashier at his father's store when he was seven years old. He had to stand on an orange crate to reach the cash register, but he learned the family business at the checkout counter when he was just a little boy.

Working alongside his or her parents is the ideal setting for a child to see the family's values in practice. We all learn better from seeing an example than from hearing a sermon. This is another great incentive for parents to practice what they preach.

Working alongside their children is an excellent way for parents to determine whether the children have the aptitude for or an interest in the business. If the children are not interested in the operation of the business, the parents can encourage them to prepare themselves to be the company's CPA, attorney, or marketing consultant, if those fields are of greater interest to them.

12. **The family requires children who will work in the business to have an education that will benefit the business.**

Time and money spent on education is never wasted if the student uses that education in a productive manner. A child who intends to work in the family business should be educated so that he or she is more valuable for the company. Even those who work in low-tech businesses can benefit from formal training.

Formal education can be helpful for day-to-day operations. It also teaches people how to think and deal with issues in a logical manner. Students are exposed to different perspectives and this helps them to realize that there are more ways to deal with problems than "Dad's way."

Most family members who are involved in the business would benefit from some college-level classes in marketing, accounting, and business management. These classes could even be taken at night after normal business hours.

13. **Children who will work in the family business are required to work for another business for a period of time.**

Every business has its own way of operating. Exposing the children to another way of doing things can prove valuable when they return to the family business. It opens the door to creative and innovative solutions that would never have been discovered in any other way. This experience can also show the children how wonderful it is to work in their own family's business as opposed to someone else's.

There is always the possibility that a child will want to stay with the other business, but that is a risk worth taking. Most parents want what is best for their children, and if working in the family business is not best for a particular child, wise parents will support the child's decision to work elsewhere.

14. Mentors are used to develop family members' abilities.

The founder of any successful business has unique talents and abilities. If not, the business would not have succeeded. These abilities are not necessarily shared by other family members. Often, the greatest talent of the founder is in utilizing and coordinating the expertise of nonfamily advisors or mentors to benefit the company and ultimately the family.

We worked with a man who had a very profitable company. He expressed a desire to take more personal time and still ensure that his children would inherit a successful company. He selected professionals to help him in the business. At the same time, they mentored his teenage children so that they could ultimately take over the family business.

A mentor is especially helpful when the founder is in the process of training his successor. Mentors can bring a perspective to the business that no family member has. A mentor typically has a talent or experience that is missing in the family business successor.

Choose a mentor who

- Understands the family values,
- Is willing to work within the constraints of the family values,
- Has the ability to train family members,
- Has expertise that is necessary for the success of the business, and
- Can be trusted.

The selection of a mentor is not an easy task. To be effective, the mentor must be trusted by both the founder and the successor. Developing trust takes time. There are no shortcuts. Business owners must begin to select mentors as soon as they determine that the business is worth passing on to the next generation.

15. Nonfamily managers are used in the absence of qualified family members.

Simply because a person is the spouse or child of a successful business owner does not mean that he or she has the ability or interest to run the family business. Business acumen is not genetic. This does not mean that family members should not take over the family business from the founder. It means that if there is no family member qualified for a position, hiring a nonfamily manager is a wise choice. This philosophy has served well the family business empires of the Rothschilds and DuPonts.

For example, a successful business owner should hire a qualified bookkeeper or controller rather than just assign that position to a child or spouse. Accurate record keeping is more important to the long-term success of the business than keeping this information "in the family."

These nonfamily managers must be motivated or they will not stay with the business. Most families do not want to give up stock because that would dilute family control. One solution is to create phantom stock. Phantom stock is not ownership in the company. It is a method of calculating a bonus, based on profitability, to be shared with the nonfamily manager as an incentive for a job well done. For example, the company has a phantom stock agreement that pays the manager 20 percent of the net, after tax profit.

Sometimes, no family member is interested in taking over for the founder. Hiring a nonfamily manager can be a way for the family to benefit from a long-term income stream rather than liquidating the business. In other cases, a nonfamily manager can be essential for an owner who is ready for retirement when the heir apparent is not ready to take over.

16. The business is protected from the effects of divorce or death of the owners.

As much as we might like to ignore it, death affects every business, and divorce affects many. Preparing for the certainty of death and the possibility of divorce does not mean that they will occur more quickly. It just means that when they do occur, the business will not die also.

Both the family members and the nonfamily employees depend on the success of the family business. Knowing that the business will survive regardless of changes in ownership engenders a sense of security and continuity for everyone.

One of our clients won $2 million in the lottery but almost lost his business in a very messy divorce. As distasteful as it might be, a prenuptial agreement that protects the business from divorce should be considered for the benefit of the employees. This agreement could simply state how the value of the business would be determined in the event of a divorce and that the business would not be dissolved or divided.

Divorce and death have a tendency to drain cash away from the business, so a viable contingency plan must ensure that there will be sufficient cash flow to keep the operations going without interruption. A qualified life insurance agent will be able to explain the products that are available to mitigate the death and divorce cash drain.

The family must discuss these problems in family meetings. A plan of action should be developed to deal with each scenario. Use an attorney to draft the required documents to make a smooth transition.

17. The family has a plan to deal with the death or disability of family employees.

Death and disability are always traumatic. When they traumatize the source of income for the family, they only make matters worse. There are several ways that a family business can prepare for the death or disability of the family employees through insurance and/or salary continuation agreements approved by the board of directors. Preparing for these contingencies will make the solutions much easier.

The family must meet and discuss how to handle the death or disability of family members. The alternatives and the related costs should be researched. Only then can intelligent choices be made. Waiting until death or disability occur before evaluating costs and alternatives can severely limit the options.

18. The family has identified the successor to the current president.

Someday, someone else is going to sit in the company president's chair. How well the successor is prepared for that day depends largely on how much time and effort has gone into training. Coincidentally, the president usually has only him or herself to blame if the successor is not trained.

The first step in training the successor is identifying that successor. Contrary to popular belief, it doesn't have to be the eldest son. Everyone in the organization benefits when the successor is the most competent individual and when that person is identified well in advance of the promotion. It might cause other siblings to look elsewhere for their careers, but that alternative is much better than their investing time and effort in a business that they may eventually leave anyway.

Roger worked with a company that was owned by two brothers.

The company prospered after they hired a nonfamily manager to run it for them. Rather unexpectedly, the brother who owned the most stock decided to promote his son and replace the manager. The son was very shrewd but he could not be trusted. The chief financial officer quit the day the son took over. The son's two cousins quit and sold their stock within the first year. The company has been a revolving door for qualified people ever since the son took over. The family aspect of the business died long ago because of the chosen successor.

The process of choosing the successor is a tricky one. Many things must be considered, but interest and aptitude have to be the primary criteria. Gender and closeness of familial relationship are rarely valid criteria. Most business founders want to choose their successor, but it would be to their benefit to consult with other trusted family and nonfamily advisors before making the choice. Often, the founder's judgment is clouded by emotions that only an outsider can put into perspective.

19. There is a time scheduled for the president to retire.

Sitting across from us were a mother and a son. They were discussing when the son would be able to take over the family business. They had the usual concerns about how it would impact the other family members and how the employees would respond. Mom wasn't sure that the time was right. The mother was seventy and the son was fifty!

To select a successor in the family business is admirable, but there should be a timetable. If the passing of the torch is always "sometime soon," the selection can become a source of frustration rather than motivation for the successor. To be effective, the selection of a retirement date should come soon after the selection of the successor, even if that date is ten years later.

The following is an example of what can happen when people don't plan to retire. In our bankruptcy practice, we worked with a company run by two brothers in their late sixties. Their children and

children-in-law had all worked for the business at one time or another. Most of them were very capable people who had the ability
to run the business better than the founders, but the founders would
not retire and give the kids a chance. They ran the business the way
it had been run for the preceding thirty years and they ran it into the
ground. Through the bankruptcy, the business assets were sold to the
kids and one bankrupt company spawned two healthy, thriving en-
terprises.

20. There is a plan to transfer the business to the next generation.

In addition to selecting a successor to manage the business, the
family must have a plan for selecting successors in the ownership of
the business. If you wonder why this is important, ask an attorney
who handles wills and probate. Ignoring it almost guarantees the
disintegration of the family after the death of the parents.

Transferring the business includes consideration of company control and tax planning, and providing for the security of the transfer-
ors in their old age. This task should not be undertaken without the
help of a CPA who specializes in taxation and an attorney, and consultation with the designated successor. Consulting with the company
mentor(s) will also help.

The IRS can play a significant role in the demise of a family
business that has not planned ahead. The tax bill can be substantial
if the business is a successful one. Consider life insurance policies for
tax liability and a "gifting program" to transfer stock in an organized
manner. Consult your CPA for your specific needs.

21. There is a method to determine which members of the family can work for, own stock in, or be on the board of directors of the business.

To believe that every family member can or will want to work
for the family business is unrealistic. This is particularly true for the

family business in its second or third generation. For this reason, the family must provide a fair way to determine who can work for the family business and who will be on the board of directors. In order for the business to survive, employee and director cannot be honorary positions.

Family members who are owners but who do not actually work in the business must be compensated for their ownership through dividends or similar means. The other choice would be to transfer nonbusiness, family assets to uninvolved family members in exchange for their ownership in the business.

The survival of the business, and possibly the family, requires that these issues be resolved by the family before the need arises. The family working together can achieve more beneficial results than can courts and attorneys.

22. The company has buy/sell agreements.

It is overly optimistic to assume that owners of a family business will never want to leave the business. People change; their needs and circumstances also change. If the family is going to maintain control of the family business, certain restrictions must be considered for selling company stock. A first right of refusal by the corporation is appropriate when a family member wants to sell ownership in the company. This issue is particularly important for second- and third-generation family businesses.

The best advice for writing buy/sell agreements is to have an attorney do it. All those who own a piece of the business should be involved in the process. The buy/sell agreements must provide for the disposition of ownership when one of the owners dies.

Establishing a fair price for ownership interest in a family business is difficult. Families often value the stock as low as is reasonable for estate tax planning. This value might not even be as much as net book value, which is the difference between the company's assets and liabilities. The reasons for a lower-than-net book value include the lack of marketability of the stock of a closely held company, a declining market for the product that the company produces, or a contingent liability that has not been recorded in the financial statements. Sometimes net book value, although it is verifiable, can show a value that is not high enough. For example, land next to Disneyland purchased fifty years ago would be on the books at the original purchase price rather than the true current value, which would be much higher.

23. There is control on the number and value of luxury items purchased by the business for employees.

A banker friend said that when he saw the owner of a business that is less than five years old driving a new Mercedes-Benz, he knew the business would fail. Not that the Mercedes caused the failure, but rather that the purchase of the luxury car—before the company had proven itself—was an indication that the owner was not as cautious as he should be. Our experience proves that he was right.

Roger once worked for one of the astronauts who walked on the moon. He was very charismatic and his company had great potential. Roger was equally impressed by the very expensive clothes of the vice president and that they both drove beautiful Mercedes-Benz automobiles. The business was relatively young and Roger had dreams of helping it to become a major aerospace company. It never happened. The clothes and cars were purchased before the money was earned. The company was liquidated in bankruptcy.

Families should benefit from the fruit of their labors, but to risk the company's future on the expectation that the fruit will ripen successfully and in the expected quantity is foolish. The benefits of a profitable business will come, and should be enjoyed by the family, after the harvest is securely stored in the silos.

24. The family has a network of other family business owners with which they share experiences and exchange information.

Family-owned businesses employ over forty million people. They account for 60 percent of the gross national product and comprise 75 percent of all businesses in the United States. What does that mean to you? It means that you're not alone. Family businesses just like yours make up the greatest portion of every dime that is earned in the United States.

One of the big mistakes that successful family businesses make is not recognizing that they are a successful *family* business and not just a successful business. Most recognize that they are part of a particular industry and they usually participate in that industry's meetings and organizations.

Family businesses must deal with important issues that nonfamily businesses need not consider. These include family disputes, succession and family employee competency. These "fuzzy issues" are usually the ones that cause a family business to fail. They are issues that are filled with emotion. They cannot be solved easily because there usually is more than one correct answer. Sometimes the correct answer will not be considered because it is uncomfortable for the family even to discuss it.

Experience has shown us that if your family business participates in a family business organization, you will feel more comfortable in dealing with the fuzzy issues. You will find that you are not alone in having these types of problems, and that other family businesses have faced these problems and overcome them. Associating with owners of other family businesses will help you gain important insights, for example, how other owners solved a particular family problem. You can profit from the mistakes of others, and possibly avoid some of the painful experiences of your fellow family business owners.

25. Discipline is the same for family and nonfamily members.

We mentioned that MBA programs don't address family business issues because of the emotions involved. There are few more stressful or emotional occasions in a business than when it is necessary to discipline someone. The feelings in a family business are intensified because of the relationships involved. You always run the risk of the Tommy Smothers Syndrome: "Mom always liked you best."

These are the key things to remember: Disciplinary measures should concentrate on helping the individual to perform better, not on breaking that person into submission. A standard written policy of progressive discipline is essential so the employees recognize that there is equity. To develop a new generation of leadership in a family business, the next generation must receive positive and effective discipline.

Our father was a strict disciplinarian at home. Let's just say that we might receive more than a tongue lashing, depending on the severity of the infraction. While working one summer in the drugstore Dad managed, Russ had the compulsive urge to practice his penmanship and label the entrance to the large trash area in the stockroom. It was just a piece of plywood that blocked the doorway and no customer would ever see it, but it happened that Dad had just painted it to cover the graffiti that others had left. Russ was there when Dad discovered the fresh black ink. The other employees tried to protect him but it was evident that the word "GARBAGE" was written by a thirteen-year-old boy. Russ thought he was doomed. He got a serious lecture and had to clean it up, but nothing else was ever said. His psyche and rear end were both glad that Dad acted as he would with any other employee.

26. **Responsibility and authority of nonfamily managers is not undermined.**

Krista was a dedicated employee of a family business for many years. Her devotion earned her a place of trust as the assistant to the president. Upon his untimely death, it would have been easy for the remaining family members to dismiss this nonfamily employee, but they chose instead to reward her with even greater responsibility. She has since repaid the family many times over with her skill at managing the business.

You have created a structure and hired a nonfamily manager because some skill is lacking among family members. If the authority of that manager is undermined in favor of a family member, you run a strong risk of losing a very valuable link in your business structure. Family relationships are important but they cannot replace learning and experience.

Remember your family values. Plan. Train your employees. Treat everyone the way you would like to be treated. Create a legacy. Refer to "How to Use This Book" in the *Introduction* as you complete this section of the Power Tools Action Plan.

Family

Item	Score	Weight	Power Tool
1		3	The family business has the four essential plans for survival, success, and succession.
2		3	The family has a mission statement for the business.
3		3	The family has a vision statement for the business.

Item	Score	Weight	Power Tool
4		2	Family values and objectives are incorporated into the strategic plan of the business.
5		2	Management knows the objectives of the family.
6		2	Family business meetings are held regularly.
7		3	Family members are competent in their assignments.
8		2	Family members are compensated according to their contribution to the business.
9		2	Performance standards are the same for family and nonfamily employees.
10		2	Family disputes are handled in a predetermined manner so as not to inhibit operations.
11		1	Children who will work in the family business start working in the business at a young age.
12		1	The family requires children who will work in the business to have an education that will benefit the business.
13		1	Children who will work in the family business are required to work for another business for a period of time.
14		1	Mentors are used to develop family members' abilities.
15		3	Nonfamily managers are used in the absence of qualified family members.
16		3	The business is protected from the effects of divorce or death of the owners.
17		1	The family has a plan to deal with the death or disability of family employees.
18		3	The family has identified the successor to the current president.

Item	Score	Weight	Power Tool
19		2	There is a time scheduled for the president to retire.
20		3	There is a plan to transfer the business to the next generation.
21		2	There is a method to determine which members of the family can work for, own stock in, or be on the board of directors of the business.
22		2	The company has buy/sell agreements.
23		1	There is control on the number and value of luxury items purchased by the business for employees.
24		1	The family has a network of other family business owners with which they share experiences and exchange information.
25		2	Discipline is the same for family and non-family members.
26		2	Responsibility and authority of nonfamily managers is not undermined.

2

Marketing:
To Make It, You Gotta Market

This section will not teach you how to write ad copy, how to be creative, or how to motivate your sales staff. There are other books designed to do that. The purpose of these marketing Power Tools is to help you increase the income of your business. After all, money is the lifeblood of every business. If you're not selling, your business will die. This applies to lawyers and doctors as well as manufacturers and retailers.

Marketing is not just sales or advertising. It is the continual process of responding to demand in the marketplace and communicating your ability to satisfy that demand. Our experience as bankruptcy trustees in a once profitable, family-owned contracting company demonstrates the importance of continuous marketing efforts. For forty years the family prepared, or fabricated, and installed steel rebar. Now they were steadily losing money.

After a simple evaluation of the existing market, we identified a large demand for fabricated rebar among small contractors who would do the installation themselves. We focused greater energy on fabrication for small jobs and increased average sales in this area from $6,000 to $60,000 per month. This simple review of the market was instrumental in turning the company around. Your business may not need drastic changes but these Power Tools will help control costs and increase sales.

27. All understand that sales is their major function.

A business requires a myriad of abilities such as sales, management, accounting, and production. When a family business is small, everyone wears many hats. Mom might do the bookkeeping, answer the phones, and sweep the floors. Although each of these jobs is important, the telephones must be given priority. A phone conversation may be the first contact a customer has with the company, hence the bookkeeper in this case is also selling. Ignoring customers while you add up a string of numbers sends the message that the numbers are more important than the people who provide the money to pay your bills.

It becomes more difficult for employees to recognize the sales aspects of their jobs as a company becomes larger and more departmentalized. When working as a buyer for a government contractor, Russ was trained in the requirements of government procurement. It was often easier to satisfy those requirements than to get the best price on the goods he was buying. He understood, however, that negotiating lower prices allowed his company to charge less and thereby be more competitive. His job was more than just buying, it was saving money so the company could sell more. It is the manager's job to educate employees that their major function is to help the company sell. Without sales, there are no raw materials, no telephones, and most importantly, no paychecks.

28. Management knows the customers.

The more you know about the people or groups of people who are buying from you, the more intelligent marketing decisions you will make. Where do they shop? What do they read? Where do they congregate? What is important to them? What problems do they share? Where do they go to learn about what you do? Fancy logos or clever ads are only effective if they appear where your customers will see them. If you send messages that your customers don't care about, they won't bother to respond. If your product or service doesn't fill a need, you will have trouble giving it away.

We consulted with an optician who advertised regularly in the local paper. His ads told how skilled he was at fitting glasses and touted the quality of the lenses he sold. We suggested that he send a letter to his past clients to solicit their opinions. We learned that most of them were women, most of them came to him because of the attractive selection of frames he carried and the follow-up service he offered. They liked how their glasses fit, but that was not the most important thing to them. We found that his letter showing interest in the customers brought in more business than all of his newspaper advertising. If you don't know your clients, get to know them.

29. Management has personal contact with large customers on a regular basis.

You have something that all of your competitors want—your best customers. Your competitors will schmooze them, wine them, dine them, give them gifts, and take them to the ball game. You might have a great service, your product may be wonderful, but every customer is subject to a condition called "What have you done for me lately?" Your salespeople can handle the small customers, but the ones that really make a difference deserve personal attention. There is something special about the boss taking the time to call or come out of the office to say hi.

Our father was the manager of a drugstore. Over his career he received prizes, trips, and large bonuses from top management for being a consistently high producer. He was a dedicated manager. He filled out the reports, stocked the shelves, and motivated the employees. But the thing that distinguished him from his peers was that he stopped and talked to the customers. He would treat them to ice cream. He frequently poked his head out of the observation window in his office to say, "I'll be right down." The customers came back, often! They could have gone to the gift store or bought their aspirin at the grocery store, but at this store the *boss* went out of his way to make them feel important.

30.   Management is dedicated to quality service and products.

Think of all the junk you have purchased in your life, the egg-beater that bent, the drill motor that smokes, and every little plastic goodie and gadget that clutters your utility drawer. You were enticed to buy them for whatever reason, but any sensible person would never buy them again. The junk market is finite. You have only one chance to sell, and when the market has been saturated, you must restructure, rename, find a new product, and try to sell again. One person can make a lot of money on a fad item, but the market won't allow your children to dupe the customer a second time. Companies that last produce quality products and strive to provide excellent service.

This is not to say that you can't succeed by selling inexpensive products. If there is a market for what you are selling, you can sell more if you sell cheaper. Your challenge is to provide value, so your client receives more than expected for the price. This keeps the customer coming back year after year and generation after generation. That is a business legacy.

31.   All employees have access to appropriate promotional materials for distribution.

We often point out to our clients how hard they work at getting and keeping customers. We ask them how successful their business would be if all their employees cared as much about the business as they did.

There was a classic line on a television show: "You are only a few people away from anyone in the world." The story was about a black domestic servant family in the 1940s. When faced with the threat of losing their jobs, the man called an old friend who worked for Eleanor Roosevelt. It only took one telephone call from the first lady to shame the family's employer into keeping the family and giving them a raise. The moral is that everyone knows someone. You may have an employee whose relative would be a great customer. Make sure your employees have access to your promotional materials. If you can't afford to supply each employee with your best brochures, you should at least provide a generic business card. You are already paying your employees; now help them sell for you.

32.   The company has a written marketing plan.

Russ was brand new as the marketing manager of a diamond abrasive tool manufacturing company. The owner assured Russ that he had complete control of all marketing responsibilities for this subsidiary. Corporate headquarters were in another state. Russ was approached by a magazine publisher to advertise. He did all his homework. The magazine had strong circulation among the target customers. The price for a full back-page ad was less than the cost of sending each subscriber a direct mail piece. Appropriate copy was available, so there would be no production cost. They had the budget to pay for an extended run. Russ approved the advertisement and monitored the inquiries from the ad. Russ's boss came unglued. He said the magazine didn't have the image he was trying to project. But it turned out that over the next two months the magazine received more inquiries from that ad than any other advertisement. By the end of the year, Russ had increased domestic sales by 19 percent and doubled profitability.

This conflict with the owner could have been avoided if there had been a written marketing plan. Never spend any money on promotion unless you know whom you are trying to reach, what you have to tell them, what activities and media they will respond to, how much money you are willing to spend, and how you are going to spend it over time. Put the plan in writing to minimize conflict.

Here are the objectives a good marketing plan can accomplish:

1. Focus your energy.

   As the owner, you may be your best salesperson, but you have hundreds of other things to do. A marketing plan should help you invest your energy where you will receive the greatest return.

2. Increase the number of people you reach.

   Your plan should include what you want your employees to do to help promote sales, what advertising media you will use, and what you will try to prompt your allies to do. The more people you have selling for you, the more people you will reach.

3. Coordinate your efforts.

   Your message will have more impact if it is the same in all media. Your sales reps should send the same message that is sent on radio, television, and in print. The plan should inform your employees and allies what you are promoting and when. The only way you can accomplish this is by preplanning.

   For example, most of us hate taking a coupon to a store and then being treated like a second-class citizen begging on the street corner. Either the clerks don't know anything about the offer or they treat you like some skinflint. You send out coupons to attract new customers. It costs a lot of money to get someone to purchase from you the first time. When you get them to bite, treat them right. Let your employees know what you are offering and when. Then treat the newcomers as if you want them to come back. Don't overuse coupons or your margins will narrow and all you will get is skinflints.

4. Minimize expense.

Your marketing plan should focus on the best means of communicating your message. Don't be seduced by advertising salespeople. Your marketing budget gives you a good excuse when they come calling. Tell them to leave their information and you will consider them in next year's budget. You still have the freedom to use a great new idea, but the budget requires you to make a conscious decision: What are you willing to give up in order to spend money on this new idea? Because the plan includes all promotional expenditures for an entire year, you can negotiate volume discounts and not pay for premium spots.

33. The marketing plan includes quantifiable markets.

We don't know how many donut stores and restaurants we have seen start up and fail after just a short time. You have heard that sales is a numbers game. If there aren't enough reachable people, with enough money, who need what you have to sell, what makes you think you can make a living selling it? You also need to know how many potential customers are out there so you can determine how to spend your advertising budget.

Many of our clients have customers in a specific area of town, either because of income level or location of their store. Such was the case with our optician friend. He was advertising city-wide in the local paper. He was paying to reach everybody to whom the paper was delivered, but his target market was affluent females. We determined that a targeted approach was more cost effective. He could advertise in a section of the paper designed to zero in on the area of town where his target market lived. The cost was greater per paper delivered, but the overall cost was less. Identify the number of potential customers in your target market so you can determine whether there is sufficient return for your marketing investment.

34.   The marketing plan is reviewed regularly.

A marketing plan is not a trophy to be displayed proudly on a shelf, or a paid invoice to be filed. It is a working document. You prepared it to last over a period of time. Do you expect everybody to remember everything that is in it?

Russ got the idea from his retail background to use a time-line approach for marketing plans. Retail stores have to plan in advance so they can order early enough to receive seasonal merchandise in time. Some things are ordered six months in advance. You should plan your advertising as soon as you know what you have to sell and when you are going to sell it. It's easy to forget about Christmas when it is 105 degrees outside.

Marketing is a continual process. We prepared a plan for a catering client. This plan started off with a bang! We upgraded his logo, identified his markets, started greater community involvement, and let everyone know about his service with press releases and local trade shows. The owner got a lot of new business and paid for everything we had done in a few weeks. He was very happy, but determined he could take it from there. He could have, but he shelved the plan and coasted. Originally he wanted to achieve a million dollars in sales, but he was satisfied after a short burst of new business. He is still doing well, but he never achieved his million-dollar goal, and he never will.

35.   The marketing plan identifies the target markets.

When you think about target markets, what do you picture in your mind? We see a dartboard. The circle in the middle earns the most points and each larger circle thereafter less and less. Your primary target market may consist of a very few people, but they will bring you the greatest return. You should invest more resources reaching them than reaching the less profitable customers. They are usually found in a larger population who are also worth your time to reach, but will not bring you as much money. Identify your target markets so everyone knows how much should be invested to reach each group.

We work with a consortium of companies that sell to school districts. They joined forces so they could share leads and booth space at trade shows. They operated for several years with this loose organization. After some analysis, we pointed out that most of their business came from medium-sized school districts. The large districts were wonderful to have as clients because they had large orders and a lot of money, but they were not influenced by promotional materials. Their business had to be personally cultivated. Small districts were a potential for business, but their small orders didn't justify a lot of effort to reach them. There were few enough large districts that the member companies could visit them, and the small districts would be reached by bulk advertising. Our primary target market, as a consortium, we believed, should be medium-sized districts. We developed several tactics to reach them.

36. The marketing plan includes a detailed budget.

No matter how small your business or how much you hate working with numbers, prepare a budget for your marketing expenditures. Many advertising people use 10 to 15 percent of gross sales as a benchmark for advertising expenditures. That is the average of what companies spend, not necessarily an optimum. First, write down what you are going to do to increase sales. Then write down what media will be necessary to support what you are going to do. Now go back and apply a dollar amount to each media and activity. Example: You are going to a trade show. You will need a display. You may want to give something away at the show, such as promotional pens or sports bottles. You will have travel, meal, and booth costs. Go back and apply a budget for each item. Include each cost on the monthly time line, where you will need to make the expenditure.

When all of your activities are listed by month, add up the months and total the year. You now have a budget. If the budget is too high, reduce it by eliminating items or stretching the activities over a longer period of time.

37. Advertising is focused on the target market.

We cringe every time we hear the phrase "You've got to get your name out there." The objective is too ambiguous. Given enough time and money, you could get your name in front of every man, woman, child, and highly developed monkey in the world. That could be wonderful, but who has enough time and money? Invest your resources where they will yield the highest return. Think of the bull's-eye on the target. Those are the people you want to reach. Other people will see and be influenced by your promotional material, but it should talk to your target customer.

We carry in our bag of tricks an advertisement that we clipped out of the local paper. It read, in big bold print at the top, "PUBIC NOTICE." At first glance, you might not notice the "L" missing from the word public. It was an ad for a nursery that was having a big sale. They obviously wanted every member of the PUBIC to know about it. If we had owned the nursery, we would have negotiated for some free advertising from the paper for making such an embarrassing error. We would also have taken a more targeted approach. Not everyone in the public was interested in a plant sale. Besides, people don't read every word in the paper, they scan the headlines for what is interesting to them. The ad looked more like a bankruptcy auction notice. A more targeted headline would be "PLANT LOVERS" or "FRUGAL FERTILIZERS." You should use terms with which your target market will identify.

38. Advertising cost is evaluated by the lowest cost per target market contact.

The effectiveness of whizbang, flashy, blowout type advertising is short-lived. It can be costly and inspires only those people who perceive a clear and pressing need to buy. To enjoy long-term success, you must reach your target markets on a consistent basis so your service is in front of potential customers when they perceive the need. Remember, 'frequent is better than flashy'. Use this formula: Ad price (P) divided by the number of target market contacts (C). Using the following data, which can normally be obtained from the advertising medium, here is an example:

Number of single males age 25 to 50 in target area = 5,000

Newspaper circulation = 80,000

Percent of circulation that are single males 25 to 50 = 5% or 4,000

Cost of newspaper ad = $2,800

Cost of direct mail, 1,000 or less = $750; 1,000 to 3,000 = $1,650; 3,000 or more = $3,000.

The cost per target market contact for newspaper advertisement is $2,800 ÷ 4,000 = 70¢.

The cost for direct mail is $3,000 ÷ 5,000 = 60¢.

In this case, even though the direct mail expenditure is greater, the cost per contact is less.

39. Unplanned promotional costs are reviewed by management for focus and return on investment.

A written marketing budget gives the owner the ability to delegate with confidence. You only have to make the expenditure decision once. As long as your subordinates follow the plan and do not exceed the budget, they can operate autonomously. Plans are not laws written in stone, they are guidelines. If some clever salesperson presents a suggestion that is not in the plan, it should not be immediately discounted or accepted. It must be evaluated. A good manager should always be open to a better idea. Have the subordinate review the cost per target-market contact and present why the new idea is better than what is in the plan. This will reduce your time investment and allow you to make a better decision.

40.   Management has defined an image for the company.

Building a family business is much like raising a child. When your first child is born, no one hands you an instruction manual. You do your best based on your education and experience and hope the kid turns out OK. If you start with a vision of the kind of person you want your child to be, it will help you make decisions along the way. Here's an example. You would like your child to become a responsible adult. This vision will lead you to help your child accept responsibility. You may give Junior chores or buy him a pet. You will not allow him to shirk his homework assignments. These things may cause you extra work, but in the long run they will help your child become the person you envisioned he or she would be.

If you develop a vision of what you want your company to be, it will help you make management decisions as well. Let's say you want Brady & Sons to be the largest widget maker in the United States. This will impact what kind of logo you select. It might not be sufficient to have cousin Katy make a pencil sketch of a Brady widget. You will require typeset flyers, not hand-printed messages on yellow copy paper.

IBM goes so far as to require even repair people to wear a white shirt and tie. Your image is a reflection to the world of the kind of organization you are.

41.   The image is appealing to its target customers.

You do not have to be a stuffed shirt to succeed in business. Our friend is an accountant. He worked for one of the Big Six accounting firms. Accounting firms present the image that they are all business: functional decor, black on white business cards, conservative ties, and so on. The two major industries our friend served were oil and agriculture. The people in these industries are typically not your big-city, "let's do lunch" types. They prefer to be unfettered by established patterns of dress. Our friend went to visit one of the firm's larger clients. The client was a successful farmer with huge land holdings. He told our friend that if he ever came to the farmer's office wearing a tie again, he would cut it off. The firm no longer has an office in that city, but our friend retained this farmer in his private practice.

The moral of this story is: The image that *you* desire is less important than the image that appeals to your target customers.

42. The image is portrayed in all promotional materials.

Country clubs appeal to a human desire for conspicuous consumption. We want other people to believe that we are successful, happy, and enjoy the life of leisure. A local country club sponsored a membership drive through the chamber of commerce. This is a reasonable target market, but the flyer they used was obviously produced on a personal computer and copied on cheap blue paper. This approach would have been expected from a janitorial service, but the professional with aspirations to grandeur would not be encouraged to join such a club. The owners obviously wanted to save money, but what is the cost of not attracting any new customers?

43. The image is reflected in the company premises.

More and more warehouse retail stores are springing up. The image is cheap. "Our products are so cheap we don't even bother to put tile on the floor or cover the air conditioning ducts. We sell tires, groceries, and lingerie; anything we can buy cheaply. Cheap, cheap,

cheap." People go to these stores seeking bargains because that's what the image portrays.

Even businesses that never deal with the public can benefit from reflecting their image in the company premises. We have monitored the growth of a knee brace manufacturer. They started in a small, garage-door-type facility. They had to be very careful that their clients didn't see their building. It didn't present the proper image for selling a state-of-the-art apparatus. When they grew out of that building, they found real estate befitting their product line. Their new facility is now pictured in their promotional materials and the salespeople are happy to invite potential buyers to visit.

Your facility can also assist you with internal marketing. A high-profile facility can attract more qualified employees and give current employees a sense of pride in where they work. Civic leaders publicly recognize citizens who enhance the beauty of their community with attractive real estate. Local news media often feature a fine-looking building as a backdrop for positive public interest stories. Even the most modest business can enhance its image by keeping the building exterior painted, the grass mowed, and the plants watered.

44. The image is fostered by all employees.

You have come to Chez Pierre to celebrate your twenty-fifth anniversary. The essence of rosemary and shallots sizzling in real butter makes your mouth water as a lovely young woman escorts you to your favorite table. You pass the semiprivate booths draped in teal and peach fabric and hear a harpist play old English folk tunes in the background. The linen tablecloth reaches just to your leg so it doesn't cling to your clothing as you slide into your seat. Then a striking middle-aged man with salt-and-pepper hair approaches to take your order. As he fills your water glasses, you notice the chain that connects his earring to the diamond stud in his nose and the quaint little studded dog collar that accessorizes his right wrist. What is wrong with this picture?

You work hard to develop an image that is pleasing to your clients. Your employees should reflect that image in their appearance and demeanor.

45. Promotional media are appropriate for the product or service.

We had a client who sold public financing services. The father-and-son team had the interests of their clients at heart. They were very capable, but their promotional materials were atrocious. They would write a business proposal on their personal computer, put it in a manila folder, and staple a business card to it. When a school or public works project is built, the financing can cost many millions of dollars. They were presenting their ability to handle these huge financial transactions in the same way a college freshman would turn in an English assignment. Your personal integrity or skill may not be sufficient to engender confidence in a customer.

Many contractors will give you a bid on the back of their business card. That is acceptable in most cases because the competition does the same thing. As a contractor, you could stand out from your peers by always using a bid form, but the clientele doesn't expect a glossy, four-color brochure. The medium you choose doesn't have to be expensive, but it must be appropriate to the application. Anything that represents your company to a customer, from television to a formal proposal, should be considered promotional media.

46. Promotional media follow a standard theme.

Each medium you use in your promotional mix may have a different purpose but should follow a standard theme. Landscape architects may choose television to show the beautiful gardens they create. Frequent radio advertising may be more affordable to create name recognition. When customers are ready to buy, they look in the yellow pages. The yellow-page ad should show the company name prominently and tie in the theme of any television and radio advertising. This is where logos and slogans become important. A simple slogan like "Tawna's Landscaping . . . for your home outside your home" should be repeated in each medium. This will help the target customers remember *your business* when they have a need for your services.

47.   Promotional media are informative yet not overly wordy.

Successful marketing is really just applying common sense. Do your clients have the time or inclination to read several pages of text about you? Today's buyers are inundated by junk mail, magazines, and newspapers. Be considerate of their precious time; get to the point.

You may determine the need for a hierarchy of information. Your first contact with a client may be a business card or a newspaper advertisement. Next you may choose to send a letter or flyer. When the clients show some interest in the product, they may require more detailed information that will build trust in your company. If you give out everything up front, you don't have an excuse for another contact.

We have been in hundreds of homes and businesses and have yet to see an extensive library of promotional materials. We have seen companies give out very expensive brochures only to have clients glance at it and throw it away. People only save the material for which they perceive an immediate need.

48.   Promotional media make it easy to see what you are selling.

Your promotional media should spark interest in what you are selling. Intangible items are the most difficult to promote. They are not like a rolling pin or a lug wrench that you can show in a picture. You have seen advertisements for financial self-help programs. They show pictures of Hawaii, or sailboats, or fancy cars. They don't often show their six audiocassettes, because that is so dull. They are selling the benefits of the program not the tapes. You might be able to talk for days about how your service was conceived or who the company president is. Cut to the chase. Show your clients how they will benefit from the services you are selling.

We just threw away an eight-page, four-color brochure. We had to review three solid pages of pictures, text, testimonials, and graphs before we figured out what the company was selling. They were selling office equipment and repair service. That's pretty straightforward. Most people don't have time to figure out what you are selling. If you can't capture their attention in five to ten seconds, you've lost them. Get their attention, tell them what you are selling, show them the benefits, and call them to action.

49. Promotional media affect as many senses as possible.

Promotional materials should impact senses, with something to feel, hear, taste, smell, and see. This is not always practical, but it's usually profitable. Russ was the assistant manager at what used to be called a five-and-dime store. One of his duties was to see that there was popcorn popping every time there were a lot of people in the store. Our culture associates popcorn with having a good time. We eat it at the movies, at carnivals, and at fairs. It has a pleasant aroma even if one doesn't like the taste. The store manager didn't care about selling popcorn; it doesn't have a great markup. He wanted the customers to enjoy their experience in the store.

Boutiques use this effectively by brewing potpourri. Aren't cookware stores more inviting when they are baking bread or, better yet, giving candy samples? The concept is to involve the client with your product or help your client relate you with a pleasurable experience. If you don't believe this works, let's do lunch.

50. All promotional media and activities are designed to satisfy the needs of the customer.

Put yourself in the place of your customer when preparing advertising or sales literature. Try to imagine what your customer would want to know about your product. Communicate your message in a manner that your customer will appreciate. One of our clients rents heavy equipment to contractors. Their customers are primarily job superintendents who work out of their trucks. We recommended a product offering and price list on a laminated three-by-five card so it would fit into a pocket and not deteriorate with moisture or use. The customers appreciated that.

We have seen and heard many promotional pieces that barely talk about the product being sold. They concentrate on the owner or inventor. It's a life story or résumé of his or her great accomplishments. An advertising salesperson only has to sell one person: you. Don't allow him or her to play on your ego. You can get your strokes when the sales start pouring in.

51. No conflicting logos or insignia are distributed.

Family-owned businesses are notorious for distributing multiple logos. Grandpa started the business and when Dad took over he wanted to create a new look. Cash was tight so the changeover wasn't complete. Maybe in the developmental stages of your image, multiple logos were created; the brothers liked this one and the sisters the other. To keep peace, the family uses both. Whatever the reason, multiple logos are bad business.

It is a waste of resources to perpetuate the use of more than one logo. Worst of all, the customers can be confused by the conflicting images. We were consultants for a construction company that had two offices, in different cities. Each was managed by a brother. Their contracts were large and numerous. They had the trucks and equipment of a large firm, but did little together because there was no unity between the two. Each brother wanted to promote his office and they developed different logos. Their advertising production costs were doubled because ads were done separately for each location. They had the ability to cooperate and do larger jobs, but the large prime contractors that worked in both areas saw them as different companies and didn't think to give them the opportunity. Ultimately the two offices were sold separately to members of the second generation. They never succeeded in becoming a big business, because everyone perceived them as separate little businesses.

52. The company is accessible to its customers.

We work with a valve manufacturer. This company has a patent on a new valve. The applications for the product are numerous, but so far the company has only addressed one market. One frustrated customer called and asked, "Are you the makers of this new valve?" "Yes," they answered. "Why aren't you in the Thomas Directory?" (This is not a plug, but the Thomas Directory is the industrial buyers' bible.) We asked the valve manufacturer the same question at our first review of their operation. We ask you the same type of question. Are you listed in the directories where your target customers expect you to be? If you are a retail store or promote will-call, are you easy to find? Do you have an 800 or 888 number? If you service other time zones, do you have a system to respond when people in those zones are working and there is no one in your office? Do your customers feel safe coming to your place of business? Do you have fax capabilities? Do you have a physical address, as opposed to a P.O. box, so you can receive returns? In short, can your customers reach you when they want you?

53. The telephone system is adequate for the number of calls received.

You can't stay in business long if you spend more than you take in. This often forces owners to make cost-cutting decisions that could hurt their marketing efforts. Remember: marketing is a continual process of communicating. If your clients can't reach you, then you are communicating that you don't want their business. Check for these things:

- Are you losing calls because of bad equipment?
- Do people get a busy signal because you don't have enough lines?
- Do you have a fax machine?
- Do you need one fax machine to send and another to receive?
- Would you get more orders if you had a toll-free number?
- Are customers cut off while on hold because of faulty equipment?
- Is there any difficulty reaching sales or customer service?
- Do customers get lost in an electronic answering maze?

If these are problems in your business, solve them before you lose another sale.

54. The telephone is answered promptly and responsibly.

We owned a temporary help service and paid a manager to operate it while we pursued our consulting practice. Most of the requests we got were for receptionists to "sit at the front desk and answer calls." That was scary to hear as a business consultant. Don't you hate to call a business and get some dingbat who can't figure out what end of the receiver to talk into? It takes five "please holds" before you can say your name and then you are cut off while being transferred. We see red just thinking about it. Your customers feel the same way.

The front desk may not merit a lot of money, but it is worth providing sufficient training. Don't stop at the front desk. Train everyone in the organization to use the telephone equipment correctly. You never know who will be answering the phone. The telephone is a powerful marketing tool in the hands of a skilled operator.

55. Initial contact is courteous and friendly.

Our grandfather Allred often quoted Will Rogers saying, "I never met a man I didn't like." Everyone he met had a fresh start with him. The new acquaintance was a friend no matter what the individual's background. Judgments were made only after personal experience. Because of the competitive world we live in, many potential customers are looking for an excuse not to use your business.

One way to keep your first impression from being your last is to smile. While working as the manager of a sales staff, Russ had one of those marginal employees who can't seem to find anything right with the customers: "They don't use the right part numbers; they don't give enough notice; they are rude." He did not deserve the title of salesperson; "salesperson" denotes a professional. He was an order taker at best. He had health problems and personal problems and problems with the other employees. In short, *he* was the problem, and sales were declining. Trying to give him every opportunity to succeed, Russ asked him if he would do just one thing: smile every time he picked up the phone. He worked the order desk for domestic sales. That year domestic sales increased 19 percent. We believe that you can hear a smile on the other end of a phone.

56. Messages are always returned.

Every call should be considered an opportunity for mutual benefit or exchange. Unreturned messages usually fall within three categories: (1) You don't know the person calling; (2) You don't want what they're selling; (3) You don't want to deal with the problem.

The demands of your business may require you to have someone else screen your calls. Even though you don't have time to talk to all salespeople who call you or you may not like to deal with customer complaints, you should not give global instructions to get rid of them all. Sales calls can be very beneficial, and customer complaints are potential new sales.

Russ does some telemarketing work for a company. Ninety percent of the messages that he leaves are never returned. If your representative says that you will return a call and you don't, that makes you or your company a liar. Russ knows of customers for whom his client could have saved hundreds of thousands of dollars, but never got the chance because a message was not returned. We have also turned a frustrated customer, on the verge of buying from our competition, into a loyal user of a more appropriate product. The difference is information.

Instruct your call screener to solicit as much information as possible and to take good notes. Preprinted message pads may not be sufficient. Tell your screener what products or services you may be interested in and what you are definitely not interested in. If there is no interest, tell the screener to decline the offer; no message need be taken.

Even though messages should be returned, you don't need to be the one to return them. With good information, you can now make good decisions as to whom you should call back. With a quick review, you can have the screener return the messages in which you have no interest. You can prepare for an opportunity to sell by researching the customer complaint and finding acceptable options. In this manner your company gains the reputation of being polite and helpful and you are informed of new and potentially profitable services.

57.   Signs are legible and obvious.

Russ received training to sell signs, and the instructor used a cartoon that had a hundred signs around a little store with a thousand customers. The caption read, "Too many signs may be in bad taste, but it's always good business." Many communities are passing strict ordinances that limit a business's ability to effectively use signs. Some businesses don't feel they need signs, because they aren't retail. To coin a biblical phrase, "Show me a sign." Look for opportunities to communicate with your potential customers. Wholesale and industrial customers drive by your place of business too. Signs enhance your company's image. Signs can also be used effectively inside a store. Unless your business is a garage sale, don't use signs that look homemade. Also consider who will be seeing your sign and from where they will see it. It's hard to read "Edward A. Balentine and Sons Home Furnishings" written on a strip mall sign when you're whizzing by at 45 mph.

A client of ours provides secretarial services in addition to its primary business. They determined not to have exterior signs because the company does very little business in town and the lease would be cheaper without a marquee sign. Still they felt there was more secretarial work that they could get. We recommended that they use a portable stake sign, like a real estate "For Sale" sign, and simply write "TYPING" on it. As people saw the sign every day on the way to work or shopping, they would remember where they could get typing done. The same hour that we drove the sign into the grass, a client stopped with ongoing needs for typing. Signs can be very powerful marketing tools.

58.   Parking is adequate.

Many shops make the mistake of choosing space because of the low rent. This may be desirable from your accountant's point of view, but your accountant doesn't have to maneuver a minivan with three kids and a golden retriever into a "Compact Only" parking space surrounded by the obligatory evergreens and ivy. Your customers' impression of you is formed long before they see the price tags. Be responsible to the bottom line, but choose a site that will accommodate as many patrons as you can serve.

59.   Pricing is as high as the market will bear.

Every entrepreneur's dream is to have a product that can be produced for a penny and sold for a dollar. The price you charge your customers should be based on their ability and disposition to buy and not on how much it costs you to produce.

Russ managed a manufacturing business that sold products to the hobby industry. They received a substantial markup even with a three-tier distribution network. They became aware of an application for a similar product used in scientific laboratories. By changing the packaging and promotion, they were able to triple the existing markup.

This strategy accommodates those industries where pricing is regulated. Your markup may be limited by statute. As a buyer for a government contractor, Russ used a "cost plus" formula to justify technology purchases that were unique and had no competition. In theory, the producers were supposed to outline costs as proof that they were not gouging the government. The way for a producer to get around that is to help the buyer justify the cost some other way. Show the alternative cost of existing products or the cost to the buyer of redesigning around your product.

60.   Demographics are reviewed annually for future market planning.

Are there enough people in your target market for you to reach the income level necessary to achieve the vision of your company?

You should answer that question affirmatively, with statistics, at least once a year. Demographics are constantly changing. We recently took over as receivers for a motel in the lower economic area of town because they didn't have enough business to repay their loan. The motel was located on a road that used to be the major highway. There were many motels along this road, but when the highway was rerouted to a freeway, all of the business from out-of-town guests went with it.

This family-owned business should have seen the writing on the wall and sold out or restructured before the city planners wielded their mighty blow. The owners might have converted the motel to an apartment complex when they had the ability to borrow money, but now the motel will probably be auctioned off and demolished for future development.

61. Sales objectives are established at least annually and identified by month.

With your company vision in mind, you should establish a gross income goal every year. That goal should be broken down into months: $10,000 in January, $15,000 in February, $3,000 in March, etc. This way you can monitor your progress in manageable increments and change your sales tactics to compensate for changes in the market.

62. Sales objectives are realistic.

"A dream is a wish your heart makes when you're fast asleep." "Somewhere over the rainbow . . ." Let's all wake up and go back to Kansas. Pie-in-the-sky objectives have no place in the real world but to frustrate and demoralize. Your company vision is your long-term objective. Your annual objectives are major steps along the way. Your major steps should be broken down into achievable goals. To reach your goals, you must start from where you are, taking into consideration where you have been.

You can gain insight into your business potential by soliciting input from your staff as to their ability to produce sales. Then increase that number slightly so everyone has to stretch a little.

63. Follow up, follow up, follow up.

We remember a Cub Scout carnival with a nail pounding booth. Several people would gather around a large block of wood and race to see who could drive a nail the fastest. This was a macho kind of thing the dads really got into. We were impressed with the professional carpenters who would start the nail with a blow, drive it with another, and set it with a third.

No offense, but customers are like blocks of wood. It's a rare individual who can drive home a point with one contact. Professionals make a contact and follow up at least three times. The follow-up can be a letter, a fax, a phone call, a gift, an advertisement, a greeting card, a skywriter, a blimp, or any combination. Set up a system that makes at least three contacts with a target customer before giving up and moving on.

64. Sales are tracked by territory.

How do you eat an elephant? One bite at a time. As a business grows, it becomes harder to control. Without established means of monitoring sales, it is impossible to adapt fast enough to changes in the market. Define logical territories, departments, product lines, industries, or markets that you can monitor and control. The obstacles will present themselves, but they are easier to handle one at a time.

65. Sales staff is friendly, knowledgeable, helpful, and courteous.

People tend to migrate to professions that suit their personalities. Hiring the right person is difficult for the most seasoned personnel manager. When hiring a salesperson, look for someone who is friendly, knowledgeable, helpful, and courteous. Don't confuse these traits with those of the stereotypical salesperson: aggressive, know-it-all, shiftless, and manipulative.

It is easier to teach a good salesperson the merits of your product or service than it is to teach a product engineer how to be a good salesperson. One of our associates says, "Hire the smile, train the rest." Russ was working a trade show booth together with a software engineer who was reluctant to sell. Russ was convinced that the engineer had the four positive sales traits. Russ suggested that he forget about being a salesperson. The engineer knew all about the product; all he needed was to be friendly, courteous, and helpful. The engineer found that very appealing. They walked the show and got a good feeling for where certain booths were located. Rather than pushing their product on the people, Russ and the engineer became traffic directors. It was very easy to ask, "What are you looking for at this trade show?" and tell the person where it was. That made the next question very natural: "Have you ever considered our service?" This casual approach helped the engineer talk to people and sell more than he thought possible.

66. Sales staff is familiar with the competition's product.

Family businesses often start family members out in sales. That is fine because they have grown up eating, sleeping, and breathing the family product. But that can also be a problem. Your sales force must have more than a passive knowledge of the competition. Salespeople have to convince potential clients of your advantage. The product includes the advertising, sales tactics, delivery, performance, packaging, customer support, price, etc. If salespeople don't know what is good and bad about the competition, they can't convey what is better about your product.

67. Sales staff takes the time to listen to the client's needs before trying to sell a product.

Our friend was a trainer for Dale Carnegie, the famous sales training organization. He would often say that most salespeople "spray and pray": get out as much information as possible before the client can tell them no and pray they've said something that sparked interest. You will be more effective if you listen to what your client needs before you try to sell something. Ask your clients enough questions to determine whether they are interested in a product. Then ask what specific features they would like. The sale then becomes easy. Tell the clients how your product meets their needs. Then confirm their decision to buy with other features they may not have considered.

68. The market for new products is examined monthly.

A great percentage of marketing is observing. Watch what people do in certain situations, consider what trends are hot, look at the advertising of other businesses, other industries. Then ask yourself every month, "Do my clients need something else that I can give them?" Capitalize on the trust that you have generated with your existing customers. If you sell home alarms, maybe your clients would be interested in personal alarms or alarms for the office. Sometimes you will identify a need that you don't feel comfortable selling. Consider teaming with another business to enhance both of your sales. Maybe you could give the other product away as an incentive to get new clients.

69. New markets for existing products are considered regularly.

There is a visual impairment called restricted fields or tunnel vision. Those who suffer from this disorder have limited or no peripheral vision. They see the world as if through a tunnel. Businesses often suffer from the same lack of perspective. Management gets caught in a rut and forgets that their products may serve other markets. The therapy for this is to look to the sides on a regular basis. At first it requires a deliberate effort, but after a while it becomes very natural. Here are some steps to help in the process:

1. Pick a day at least quarterly to think about marketing. Schedule at least an hour on your calendar.
2. Reduce your product or service into rudimentary functions. Instead of tunnel vision thinking like "Our products use diamonds to facet and polish gemstones in the hobby industry," think, "Our products grind and smooth hard surfaces quickly and economically." By considering your products in more general terms, you may see more applications for the same products.
3. Consider your existing clients and ask what they are doing with your products.
4. Visit your network of contacts and ask them specific questions about how your product might help them.
5. When you identify a potential application for your product, set goals and time limits to find answers to specific questions.

70. Market trends are examined monthly.

A primary duty of management is to plan for the future. The more an occurrence repeats itself, the stronger the trend. The stronger the trend, the more impact on future events. The examination of trends should not be limited to sales. Determine the trends that impact your business: fashion, environment, legislation, the economy, and so on. By monitoring trends on a monthly basis, you have a better chance of adapting to meet future challenges.

The employment service we owned provides a good example of this. When we started the business, we had a plan that showed profitability within six months. Everything went according to plan and we had high hopes for this blossoming company. Then the Gulf War started. Who would have guessed that something thousands of miles away would have so much impact on a small business in Central California? But we live in an area that is dependent on the price of oil and agriculture. At the same time, we were experiencing an extended drought and a recession. Major companies in the area took a cautious stance and instituted hiring freezes. Other businesses followed suit, and our sales declined accordingly.

Month after month we saw sales declining. We determined that if the trend did not reverse itself by a given date, we would shut the business down. Though we experienced large losses, we were able to save ourselves from financial ruin. Within six months we paid all our obligations by concentrating on our other business interests. All businesses have setbacks; the businesses that last keep an eye on trends and adapt accordingly.

71.   Sales trends are analyzed monthly by the sales manager.

This tool has a double edge. One, you need to analyze sales monthly, and two, you need a sales manager. In a small company everyone wears many hats. Make sure that the "hats" are distinct job descriptions and that one of those is a sales manager. By taking an average of sales each month and graphing it on a line chart, you can easily see a trend. Most industries experience some kind of seasonality, a time of year when sales traditionally fall or rise. Each month's sales should be compared to previous year's sales for that month.

There is no trick to analyzing sales. Just ask two questions: Are this month's sales higher or lower than the norm? and Why?

72.   Radical changes in trend are examined in detail.

By some genetic fluke, Russ's oldest daughter was born with above average intelligence. As a small child, her insistent inquiries often became annoying: "Why is the sky blue?" "Why is it dark at night?" "Why are you driving so fast?" "Why didn't you stop back there?" Why, why, why? We know that what adults consider normal and mundane is all new to a child. Everything is an adventure and their questions are the way they learn. As we get older, we lose interest in the ordinary and ask fewer questions. When there is a radical change in a normal trend in our business, however, we need to sit up and take notice. We need to ask more questions and not rest until we find the answers. If your sales are the same month after month and all of a sudden they jump 30 percent higher, ask why. Was it an outside stimulus or something you did internally? Why was it that month? What can we do to make it continue? Why, why, why?

73. All customer complaints are investigated quickly and completely.

One of our clients is still fuming about the way he was treated by his overnight mail carrier. He received belated notice of a request for a proposal. His firm was uniquely qualified so he spent two full days in preparing and then submitted a bid that meant at least $50,000 in business. The bid never got there. He went through the process of filing a complaint and waited for the response, and waited and waited. Two months later the company had still not even acknowledged receipt of the complaint, let alone investigated the loss. When our client finally called, he was informed that the complaint had been received and their investigation showed that the bid must have been lost in transit. Further he was told that there was nothing they could do about it and "Have a nice day." Russ can attest that the human face can demonstrate every color of red visible by the human eye.

To the carrier, the package was just cardboard with an address. To our client, it was $50,000. There are at least three purposes for investigating a complaint: one is to find flaws in your processes so the complaint doesn't happen again; two is to provide a reasonable answer to pacify your customer; and three is to make amends so the customer will use you again or at least not blab your mistake to all his or her friends.

74. Dissatisfied customers receive a courteous and personal response.

You may already agree with the adage that the hardest thing you'll ever do is get someone to buy from you for the first time. The second hardest thing is to get them to buy from you again. A lot of time and energy is spent getting new customers, but keeping them is sometimes forgotten. It is a good policy to treat a customer complaint like a potential sale. If customers called and expressed an interest in your product, you wouldn't avoid them. You would return their calls immediately, you would treat them well, you would ask how they intended to use the product, you might even make special concessions to make them happy.

Circuit City has won Russ's wife's undying loyalty or at least a lot of good word-of-mouth advertising. In her kitchen sits a brand-new refrigerator. Four years ago another new refrigerator sat there. They bought that one from Circuit City along with an extended warranty and service contract. Because the fridge required repeated service calls, the store offered to replace it with a new one. Everyone who sets foot in the house has to hear the story of the free fridge. They have convinced several people where they should buy their new appliances, and when they need something new, there is no question where they will go. If you show sincere concern for the client and stand behind your product, you won't have to go searching for new clients, because your old ones will come back again and again.

75. Selling costs are compared to gross margin on sales.

Evaluating items on a financial statement is often assigned to an accountant, but your marketing/sales manager should know how much money is being spent to earn sales and if the sales justify the cost. The gross margin on sales is gross sales, minus the material and labor costs. The difference is how much money is left to pay overhead expenses. This comparison allows the marketing manager to monitor and adjust sales strategies to reduce selling costs while increasing sales. Bankers and accountants use industry ratios to determine how well a company is doing. These ratios are useful as a benchmark, but they should not govern how you spend your advertising dollars. They are an average of what like businesses spend in this area. Your objective should be to stand out from your peers not appear just like them.

The appropriate management of sales cost to gross margin on sales should yield geometric increases. That is to say, every new dollar spent on sales should yield more than a proportional amount of income.

You can accomplish this by using the Power Tools in this section. Define lucrative markets. Focus your energies on meeting the customer's needs. Communicate effectively. Follow up. Review your work and modify your efforts to improve.

Marketing

Item	Score	Weight	Power Tool
27		3	All understand that sales is their major function.
28		1	Management knows the customers.
29		3	Management has personal contact with large customers on a regular basis.
30		2	Management is dedicated to quality service and products.
31		1	All employees have access to appropriate promotional materials for distribution.
32		3	The company has a written marketing plan.
33		2	The marketing plan includes quantifiable markets.
34		2	The marketing plan is reviewed regularly.
35		2	The marketing plan identifies the target markets.
36		2	The marketing plan includes a detailed budget.
37		3	Advertising is focused on the target market.
38		2	Advertising cost is evaluated by the lowest cost per target market contact.

Item	Score	Weight	Power Tool
39		2	Unplanned promotional costs are reviewed by management for focus and return on investment.
40		3	Management has defined an image for the company.
41		2	The image is appealing to its target customers.
42		2	The image is portrayed in all promotional materials.
43		1	The image is reflected in the company premises.
44		1	The image is fostered by all employees.
45		3	Promotional media are appropriate for the product or service.
46		2	Promotional media follow a standard theme.
47		2	Promotional media are informative yet not overly wordy.
48		2	Promotional media make it easy to see what you are selling.
49		1	Promotional media affect as many senses as possible.
50		2	All promotional media and activities are designed to satisfy the needs of the customer.
51		2	No conflicting logos or insignia are distributed.
52		3	The company is accessible to its customers.
53		2	The telephone system is adequate for the number of calls received.
54		3	The telephone is answered promptly and responsibly.

Item	Score	Weight	Power Tool
55		3	Initial contact is courteous and friendly.
56		1	Messages are always returned.
57		2	Signs are legible and obvious.
58		1	Parking is adequate.
59		3	Pricing is as high as the market will bear.
60		2	Demographics are reviewed annually for future market planning.
61		3	Sales objectives are established at least annually and identified by month.
62		2	Sales objectives are realistic.
63		2	Follow up, follow up, follow up.
64		1	Sales are tracked by territory.
65		3	Sales staff is friendly, knowledgeable, helpful, and courteous.
66		2	Sales staff is familiar with the competition's product.
67		3	Sales staff takes the time to listen to the client's needs before trying to sell a product.
68		2	The market for new products is examined monthly.
69		3	New markets for existing products are considered regularly.
70		2	Market trends are examined monthly.
71		2	Sales trends are analyzed monthly by the sales manager.
72		2	Radical changes in trend are examined in detail.

Item	Score	Weight	Power Tool
73		2	All customer complaints are investigated quickly and completely.
74		2	Dissatisfied customers receive a courteous and personal response.
75		1	Selling costs are compared to gross margin on sales.

3

Management:
Who's the Boss?

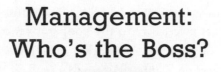

We have had some very interesting experiences dealing with family businesses in bankruptcy. Roger was appointed by the bankruptcy court to be the trustee of a manufacturing business. His first meeting with the owner was memorable. The owner was a *salesman*, bright-colored golf clothing and a grin from ear to ear. He boasted how he had increased sales in his company by millions of dollars and how this year sales would be over $22 million. "If sales are so good," Roger asked, "why is your company in bankruptcy?" The owner responded that the bank would not renew his line of credit, but he was confident that he could find alternative financing. Sadly, his overall financial condition did not merit financing and no one was willing to loan him any money. Roger was forced to liquidate the business. Why was a company with such robust sales in such a woeful financial situation? The reason was that the owner was selling but he was not collecting!

The owner of a business has to do more than just sell or produce or account. Business owners must manage all aspects of their business. A business owner is a general who must marshal the forces to win the economic war. The following management Power Tools will help you to focus on what must be done and what must be done now.

76. Management directs the business in a positive manner.

There are as many different management styles as there are managers. Some are totally autocratic and some totally cooperative in nature. Most management styles lie somewhere in between the two extremes. The autocratic style was by far the most popular in the last century. It has given way to the cooperative style for a number of reasons. One of these reasons is that laws have been passed that give employees certain rights that could not have been imagined a hundred years ago.

Probably the most important reason that cooperative management styles have increased in popularity is that they work! Employees are people, and people work best when they feel important and a part of the team. A strong leader is important to the success of a business but a strong and *positive* leader can accomplish much more. An added bonus is that a positive leader can rely on employees to work in a positive manner even when the leader is not around to personally direct the work.

77. Management is dedicated to long-term profitability.

The bankruptcy courts are crowded with businesses that made money at one time or another. Practically any business can show a profit for a short period, but forcing short-term profits can cause the ultimate failure of the business. Roger lived in Peru in the early 1970s, shortly after a new revolutionary government had taken the cattle ranches away from the owners and given them to the workers. Everything was fine for a short time, but then there was no beef in the marketplace. In an attempt to enjoy the benefits of their new-found status as cattle ranchers, the workers had butchered the breeding stock—short-term profit, long-term disaster.

Even well-established businesses fall victim to overlooking the impact of their choices on the long-term viability of the business, in an attempt to satisfy the short-term desires of stockholders or spouses or children. The business whose management takes the "long view" is the only one that has the potential of creating a legacy. Others may show flashes of brilliance, but in the end they burn themselves out.

78. Management's integrity is beyond reproach.

Business integrity is considered by some to be an oxymoron. Our experience has given us a different opinion. Granted, we have known people who lack integrity who are successful in their businesses, but we have known many, many more who have failed miserably. Included in these failures due to lack of integrity are most of the companies Roger has managed as a bankruptcy trustee. No one wanted to deal with them because they could not be trusted. The currently successful who lack integrity run the risk of the same fate.

Integrity cannot be imitated or faked or put on and off like an overcoat. It must be lived in every aspect of one's life. This would include how members of management treat their family, neighbors, and anyone else. Integrity also includes how observant we are of laws, including the truthfulness of our tax returns. Only managers with integrity can inspire their employees to act with integrity. When both management and employees act with integrity, it unleashes a powerful force that makes success much easier to attain.

79. Management is goal oriented.

How much fun would watching football be if there were no goal line? No one could ever tell whether a team was successful. The same principle applies to business. Goals help managers determine whether their choices are bringing the company nearer to success.

Management must never expect more from its employees than it expects from itself. Therefore, if employees are expected to reach specified goals, management should hold itself accountable for at least the same level of expectation. And a reward system for reaching goals should be applied to both management and nonmanagement staff. Only then is management truly goal oriented.

80. The company has a logical organization.

As in the famous Abbott and Costello routine, we want to know "Who's on first?" People do much better in an organization if they know who is in charge and who is their immediate supervisor. A person can only serve one master well. If we want employees to meet the expectations of the boss, the employees need to know who really is the boss.

Every organization, especially a family business, needs to have a legitimate organizational chart. A legitimate organizational chart will show things as they really are instead of how they ought to be. In short, if Mama has to approve every major transaction, then the organizational chart should show Mama's rightful place in the organization.

81. The company has written standards and objectives.

If your receptionist were to be consistently ten minutes late for work, could you point to a policy or directive that states that employees have to be to work at a specific time? We know of employees who have used this argument when faced with disciplinary action. Putting your standards and objectives in writing is a hassle but it leaves no room for doubt.

In addition, if having "zero defects" is important for you as the boss, you must communicate this priority to your employees. They might think that a large number of units produced with a "few defects that we can fix if we have to" is what management really wants.

People are more likely to hit the target if they know what the target is.

82. Responsibility is delegated to the lowest level possible.

Delegation to the lowest competent level of personnel is the best way that any manager can maximize the effectiveness of his or her organization. Truly effective managers know that they must delegate, and they know how to delegate. In order to properly delegate, you must first come to the realization that you are not the only competent person in your organization and, second, you must accept that a job can be done correctly even if it is not done exactly how you would do it. If you cannot accept these two axioms, delegation will always be frustrating.

Some people believe that they are good at delegating, but they never seem to get the desired result. Perhaps it is because they are not really delegating. They are, instead, engaging in the age-old tactic of "drop the bomb and run." Delegation is an art form that involves using good judgment, consistency, follow-up, and most of all, people skills. Delegation will not make all our problems go away. It is a method of systematically training employees to accomplish the tasks that are the most important.

This is an acrostic that outlines the steps to better delegation:

- Determine who should do the job.
- Express confidence in their ability.
- Let them know what you expect.
- Establish a negotiated deadline.
- Get a commitment to the job and the deadline.
- Allow them to use their imagination and initiative.
- Train them by following up, not taking over.
- Express appreciation for actual results.

Consistently applied, these delegation techniques will inspire your staff to excellence and will allow you more time to do what only you can do!

83. Delegated authority is not superseded without absolute need.

Roger once had a boss who would hire the best CPAs, attorneys, and employees that money could buy and then ignore their advice. He was a better accountant than the accountants and a better attorney than the attorneys, at least in his own mind. This not only wasted his money, but it also diverted his attention from his job as the president of the company. Since no one could do anything as well as he could, he was trying to do everything, and everything he did was done poorly.

Superseding delegated authority strips the delegates' ability to be effective, diminishes their confidence in themselves, and stifles trust in the person who superseded their authority. Hence, it should never happen, unless the results otherwise would be catastrophic. And then the boss should explain why the person's delegated authority had to be superseded.

84. Management support of supervisors is apparent to all.

Supervisors are selected because they have the skills to motivate others to perform at an optimum level. These supervisors can only be effective when they know, and everyone else knows, that the boss supports them. The boss would be well advised to let everyone from employees to vendors know that management has confidence in its supervisors. Doing anything else would be contradictory to the logic of having supervisors.

85. The company has regular management meetings.

Many people regard meetings as just a way to avoid the real work or as a waste of time. Many meetings are a waste of time, but they do not have to be. An effective meeting can save millions of dollars and thousands of hours in pursuing objectives that are inappropriate.

Regular management meetings can be used to accomplish short-range objectives, such as determining the current week's strategy. Or they can be used to address more long-term objectives, such as to reaffirm the goals, mission, and vision of the company. The difference between an effective meeting and a "waste of time" is not the meeting, it is the ability of the one in charge to make the meeting productive. Regular, effective management meetings are an essential element of prosperous and growing companies.

One of our clients used to have meetings only when there was a disaster. They now have scheduled Monday morning management meetings. We believe that the decrease in the number of their disasters is not just a coincidence.

86. The company has regular staff meetings.

No doubt everyone has heard employees referring to themselves as "mushrooms" because management keeps them in the dark and feeds them a lot of manure! Since mushrooms are not known for their productivity, management should have regular staff meetings.

Staff meetings have two major functions: first, to keep the staff informed about the objectives of the company and the company's progress in achieving those objectives; and second, to get the staff's perspective about what needs to be done. An "all employee meeting," held twice a year, improves morale and builds a better employee team.

87.   All suggestions are noted and carefully considered.

The best way to stop the flow of ideas on how to improve the company is to ask for suggestions and then ignore them. This does not mean that management has to implement all ideas submitted. It does mean that management must take note of the suggestions and then carefully consider them. Most ideas for increased productivity will come from the bottom up and not from the top down. It would be a shame to miss those ideas because management did not act interested in what the employees had to say.

88.   Ideas are acted on quickly.

It is exciting to work for a company that quickly acts on good ideas. Employee morale is enhanced by a quick follow-up on suggestions. If an employee wants a 100-watt bulb in the storeroom rather than a 75-watt bulb, to make it more safe, a quick lightbulb purchase can generate a great deal of goodwill with the entire staff.

Some ideas will require more time to evaluate. For example, if an employee suggests building a satellite distribution facility, the commitment of company resources requires careful analysis. The higher the cost, the more time and energy should be invested in evaluation.

89.   "Trials" are not held to place blame for mistakes.

We know of only one man who was perfect. Most of us fit into the category of those who make mistakes. We like the concept that people should be praised in public and reprimanded in private. Sadly, some managers feel that they need to focus as much attention as possible on someone who has made a mistake. Now, *that* is a big mistake. Mistakes should be dealt with quickly and humanely. People who continue to make the same type of mistake should be terminated rather than subjected, along with everyone else, to the humiliation of constant criticism.

90. Managers "wander around" to keep in touch with employees.

We recently completed an "employee satisfaction survey" for one of our clients with over one hundred employees. A common request was to see the general manager in the plant more often. They didn't need him there to tell them what to do but rather to interact with them. They wanted to know that he really knew what was happening in the plant and that *he cared*. This concept of managers wandering around was made popular by Tom Peters. It wasn't a new, revolutionary management technique; it was just based on what employees need and want.

91. Management expects good performance.

Being a manager and being a parent have a lot in common, especially if you are the parent of teenage children. Realistically, you know that you cannot make them do what you want, you can only encourage good behavior and impose sanctions for disobedience. As Roger tells his kids, "You don't *have to* do what I tell you. There are only two things you *have to* do: die and pay for your sins." Employees don't have to do what they are told either. But they are subject to the sanctions of progressive discipline and eventual termination.

Management must communicate to employees that good performance is expected. *Expecting* good performance is much more motivating than *demanding* good performance. An expectation of good performance implies confidence that the employees are capable of doing exactly what you want them to do. A demand of good performance, on the other hand, creates a potential ego conflict. The difference between expecting and demanding can be best illustrated by these two statements: "I expect you to do a good job because you know what needs to be done and how to do it," compared to "You are going to do it because I said so!" Employees, children, and everyone else will respond much more favorably if they know that good performance is expected rather than demanded.

92.   Staffing levels are reviewed regularly.

Employees are the largest single cost in the income statements of most businesses. Uncontrolled payroll and related costs have forced more than one business out of business. As with any large cost of operation, managers have the responsibility of monitoring and reducing payroll costs whenever it is prudent. If work is seasonal, then payroll costs need to reflect the seasonality. When demand for the company's product or service is up, payroll should follow, and vice versa. Allowing employee costs to self-correct in an economic downturn can be for many businesses the last fatal decision.

93.   There is little excess personnel capacity.

As Roger was considering working for a large farming operation, one of the managers told him, "I like to keep the workload at about 150 percent for every employee." Roger turned down this job opportunity because the manager was a fool. About a year later the manager was removed from his position because of his incompetence. Worker overload creates stress, errors, absenteeism, turnover, workers' compensation claims, and sometimes lawsuits.

Workload should approximate staffing as closely as possible. It is as foolish to make radical reductions in staffing for a temporary downturn as it is to make no reductions for a permanent downturn. Ideally, personnel should be fully utilized, with just enough excess capacity to handle vacations and illness.

94.   Overtime is planned and controlled.

Paying overtime is a practical approach to a temporary upswing in business, if properly monitored. It should not be left to the employees' discretion, because overtime can always be justified by someone who wants the overtime premium. Managers need to calculate the break-even point for hiring another employee and then hire at that point. All overtime should be preapproved by management.

95.   Decreases in staffing levels are handled fairly and with extreme care.

Encouraging productivity gains and then firing good employees if productivity does increase leads to a loss in productivity. Use those productive employees elsewhere until demand catches up with production. Unless it is necessary for survival of the business, employees should only be terminated for poor performance. Even then, management needs to be very cautious and follow predetermined termination procedures. Every effort should be made to assist good employees in finding a new job. Considering that the average wrongful termination lawsuit award approximates $1 million, the need for fair and careful handling of terminations should be self-evident.

96.   Excess files, computer programs, procedures, etc., are identified and eliminated.

The words "cluttered" and "efficient" rarely can be used to describe the same business. An associate of ours described going to his attorney's office and finding papers stacked six inches deep over the attorney's entire desk. Client's files covered the floor except for a path to the attorney and the client's chairs. "But," said our associate, "he was able to put his hands on my file without any problem." We are not impressed by someone who is able to "manage the mess."

No matter how brilliant this attorney might be, he would get more done and make fewer mistakes if he were organized. The same applies to people who keep computer programs, files, and policies that are no longer in use. Efficiency gains will far outweigh that rare occurrence when you wished that you had not thrown something away.

97. The company is not a victim of "paralysis through analysis."

One of the biggest advantages that a small- to medium-sized company has is its ability to respond quickly to changes in the marketplace. These companies look at what is happening, make a decision, and make the necessary changes. This advantage should not be lost in an attempt to be more like one of the "big boys." Remember, Ford employed four hundred MBAs for three years before introducing the Edsel. Analysis is important in making any significant decision, but once one has the facts, it is time to act. Analyze—yes! Paralyze—no!

98. The company makes a reasonable number of mistakes.

Those who never make mistakes are those who never do anything. Being prudent is wise, but every successful individual and business must make a reasonable number of mistakes. Making mistakes is part of making decisions. A lack of mistakes shows a stagnant organization that is not willing to be innovative or progressive.

99. Customers are billed immediately after delivery.

The consumer's perception is that the value of the product or service purchased decreases each day *after* the purchase. It is the manager's job to ensure that billing takes place simultaneously with delivery of the product or service. This will increase customer satisfaction and decrease collection problems.

100.   Managers take care of their personal lives.

In order to operate at peak performance, managers must do those things that maintain their personal lives. Even if you are the smartest, most talented manager of all time, if you die too young to use those talents, it really does not matter.

Few businesspeople would advocate the "peace, love, and rock and roll" hippie ideology of the sixties, but all work *does* make Jack a dull boy. The following is probably the most important checklist you can use to improve your personal life:

_____   I take time to develop deep, meaningful relationships with my family.

_____   I give something of myself to mankind through activities such as donating blood, teaching a Sunday School class, or being a Scoutmaster.

_____   I play regularly, and when I play, I play hard.

_____   I get enough rest.

_____   I eat well or supplement my diet so that I get proper nutrition.

_____   I exercise at least three times per week.

_____   I take time every day to thank God for my life and I try to draw closer to that source of life.

_____ I try to learn something new every day so that my intellect is continually stimulated.

_____ I do not use any type of recreational drug.

_____ I make a personal commitment to myself that each new day will be *fantastic*.

101.   Profit margins are sufficient for each product.

Once profit margins are known for each product, management must make decisions about which products to produce and promote. Keep in mind that a 5 cent profit margin on an item that sells a million a month is better than a $100,000 profit margin on an item that sells one per year. However, it might make sense to continue to produce and promote both. This product synergy, the way that products can help promote one another, is an important factor in production decisions.

102.   Profit margins are tracked monthly.

A good way for companies to find themselves in bankruptcy is to assume that sales and costs never change. Sales and costs do change, and the wise manager is the one who monitors these important elements on a monthly basis. Once managers are informed, they can make informed decisions to maintain or enhance the overall profitability of the company.

103.   Net margins exceed alternate investment yields.

One of our clients was sitting at the conference table with his management team. He became quite frustrated because some of the managers did not see the need to reduce costs. Finally he exclaimed,

"If we can't make more money than this, I might as well sell the business and put my money in the bank."

If your investments are yielding more than your business, sell your business. Why take the risk? In other words, why work eighty grueling hours a week to make less than if you were on the beach at Waikiki with your money in government-guaranteed certificates of deposit?

104. Major costs are identified.

The only way to defeat the enemy is to know the enemy. Costs of operation are the enemy. Every manager should be able to identify the major costs of the business. Typically, but not always, these costs will be employee related. Remember, the costs, not the employees, are the enemy.

105. Cost cutting efforts concentrate on major costs.

One of management's duties is to keep costs to a minimum. The only efficient way of doing this is to focus the greatest amount of effort on the largest costs. This does not mean that managers neglect the small savings. It does mean that the greatest effort is concentrated on the areas that have the greatest potential for savings.

One of our clients was paying an enormous sum for insurance coverage. It was a major cost to the business. We determined to go out to bid for insurance coverage, if for no other reason than to keep the broker honest. We found out very quickly that the company was paying the broker for insurance that was not typically written through brokers. The broker was just getting a piece of the action because no one had been asking the right questions. In the end, we found an equally strong insurance carrier that sold us three times as much coverage for one-half of the price! The broker is now looking for a replacement client.

106. Any change is reviewed for cost/benefit relationship.

Change for change's sake is not productive management. Every decision to make a change must include an examination of both the cost and the benefit of the change. Employee morale costs must be added to the equation when doing any cost/benefit analysis.

We attended a chamber of commerce seminar where the newly appointed chief operating officer of a successful trucking company spoke on reducing costs. The COO boldly explained the cost-cutting measures he had implemented since his appointment. The company had realized $3,500 a month in savings by eliminating the water coolers in the offices. The savings included wasted work hours socializing. Another cost-cutting measure was to move the company to another state, thus displacing many of the workers and their families. The latest news was that the company was in bankruptcy. Obviously, the benefit of the cost-cutting measures was not worth the cost.

107. Reducing costs is an ongoing effort.

Simply because a company is profitable is no justification for ignoring the importance of reducing operating costs. Costs, like rats, have a nasty way of multiplying if left alone. The ever-vigilant manager will reduce waste wherever and whenever it exists. One caution: do not be so enamored of the idea of cutting costs that once the fat is cut away, you begin cutting the muscle and into the bone.

108. No area is exempt from cost-cutting review.

Many organizations have their own sacred cows. These areas are considered off limits to cost cutting efforts. This is a big mistake. One sacred cow can eat all of the grass. This problem can be particularly acute in a family business. "That is Uncle Evan's branch office.

It would cause family warfare if we were to question why he doesn't integrate with the other offices." This big mistake has its origins in weak management that doesn't have a strategic plan. Every aspect of the business should be reviewed for potential cost savings.

109. Financial trends are examined monthly.

The financial statements that the bean counters (that is the accountants like Roger) prepare are a waste of time and effort if management does not use them. One of the best ways to use financial statements is to look at any trends they show from month to month. Monthly review of the financial data requires that the manager schedule time with the head bean counter to really understand what the financial statements mean.

110. Any change in financial trends is examined in detail.

Why are sales increasing at such a rate? Why is telephone expense so high in the winter months? Why does labor remain constant when the contract revenue decreases?

These are the types of questions management should be asking every month upon review of financial statements. The answers to these questions should be obtained quickly and in detail. Changes in trends can alert management to little problems before they can become big enough to swallow the business.

111. Large variances in any account are explained.

If expenses for travel and entertainment are increasing at 25 percent each month in brother Bryce's division, there is probably a problem. (Unless you consider playing the ponies a normal course-of-business expense.) Managers should be held responsible for reporting, or at least understanding, why there are large variances in any one of the expense categories for which they are responsible. This is the type of analysis that accountants love because it makes them feel like they actually have some power!

112. Cash flow is analyzed monthly.

To be profitable is wonderful but as the slogan goes, "Happiness is positive cash flow." It is possible to be profitable and not have positive cash flow. If profits are tied up in inventory or accounts receivable, you could be making a great profit but be unable to pay the bills as they come due. For this reason, a monthly analysis of cash flow is critical, especially for businesses that don't have a line of credit with the bank.

The owner of a profitable manufacturing company prided himself on his ability to produce inventory. The margins on his inventory were very high so he thought the more product he had the more he could sell. His warehouse was full but he had trouble making payroll. He ended up selling the business to someone who understood positive cash flow. On occasion he visits the company and comments on how little inventory they carry. The new owner just smiles and thinks about all the cash he has in the bank.

113. Cash flow is monitored daily.

It is very embarrassing, not to mention damaging to your reputation, to get a call from your banker telling you that you are overdrawn, *again*. Every business needs a system to track the current bank balance of the checking account. This can be something as simple as a check register like you have for your personal checking account. It could be a spreadsheet or a sophisticated cash management system. Whatever it is, it should work and should be used.

114.   Inventory levels are analyzed for trends.

For many businesses, inventory control *is* cash management because such a high percentage of the cash is invested in inventory. Controlling inventory levels is a management function and not an accounting function. Accountants can provide the data to show inventory level and sales trends, but management must determine how to best utilize the cash of the company when investing in inventory.

115.   Obsolete inventory is identified for liquidation.

Just as cluttered offices are inefficient, so are cluttered warehouses. The big difference is that you cannot sell canceled invoices and interoffice memos for much money. But there can be some big bucks in liquidating unwanted or unneeded inventory. Managers are sometimes reluctant to sell obsolete inventory because they will have to show a loss on the liquidation. Big deal! Get rid of it and get some cash rather than sitting on a pile of junk so you don't have to admit that maybe someone made a purchasing mistake.

116.   Inventory is purchased according to a plan.

As any manufacturer will know, to produce one hundred widgets you need all of the components of the one hundred widgets. You can't produce some that are lacking a piece or two. A production plan requires a complimentary purchasing plan. A sales plan also needs a complimentary purchasing plan. A half-empty showroom is not a productive place to make sales. Inventory needs to be purchased according to projected sales and production, not according to how great a deal you can get for buying in bulk.

117. Cash flow will support the inventory plan.

Once the production or sales plan is in place and the purchasing plan is established, management must determine if there is sufficient cash to purchase what is needed. If not, you have to work backward and modify the production plan to produce only the number of units for which you can afford component parts.

We know a man who was determined to mass produce an innovative fishing lure. He decided, against our advice, to produce a certain number of lures even though he had very little cash and relatively few outstanding orders for his product. He was sure that sales would skyrocket if he had the inventory. These sales would pay for the costs of production and he would be wealthy. Short version: he's bankrupt.

118. Carrying/handling costs do not exceed profit margins.

The true profit of a product includes more than just "sales price less cost of production." The entire equation must include the financing costs of carrying the product, not to mention the raw materials, until it is sold. If nothing else, money spent on inventory is not in the bank earning interest. Selling and general and administrative costs must also be covered by the sales price. Each product must receive its pro rata share of the carrying, selling, and general and administrative costs in order to determine if it is truly profitable.

119. Inventory is ordered for just-in-time delivery.

Just-in-time delivery is a relatively recent inventory stocking theory that has gained wide acceptance. The concept is that inventory is delivered just as it is needed, in order to reduce the carrying costs of inventory. Much has been written about this theory but this is the only thing you really need to know: it's a great idea if your inventory is delivered just-in-time.

120. Purchase orders are issued only by authorized employees.

Those who purchase in a company have a lot of power. They can make the operation run as smooth as glass or they can make life miserable. Since they have so much power, it is important that only designated people have purchasing authority and that only they can issue purchase orders. Others in the organization should issue purchase requisitions but the purchasing agent should make the actual purchases. Of course, small or recurring purchases can be put on a blanket purchase order. Centralizing purchasing authority should increase purchasing power and discounts, enhance internal control of financial commitments, and improve efficiency by having skilled purchasing agents doing the buying.

121. Purchasing is independent of operations and accounts payable.

A dishonest or incompetent purchasing manager can do some real damage to a company. Proper internal control requires that the purchasing be done by someone who has no connection to either accounts payable or production. In this way, both accounts payable and production personnel will monitor the spending of the purchasing agent. Since collusion is almost impossible to stop, management should consistently monitor the purchasing function.

122. Goods are approved as they are received.

Goods should not be accepted until they have been inspected. The person doing the receiving should compare the packing list to the original purchase order and indicate in writing that the items received are in good condition and in the quantity ordered. If not, the discrepancy should be noted on the purchase order and the purchasing agent alerted.

123. The purchase order is matched to the receiving report and invoice.

A responsible person designated by management should match the invoice to the purchase order and the receiving report. If the quantity, price, and condition are correct, the responsible person should initial the invoice as the approval for payment.

124. Competitive bids are obtained on all large purchases.

Competition is what makes the free enterprise system work. A business can not benefit from the competitive marketplace if purchases are always made from the same vendors. Management should insist that at least three competitive bids are obtained for large dollar purchases. The bid system keeps everyone honest. If the company wants to continue to buy from Auntie Alicia, even though her price is $10,000 higher than the competition, at least it will be a consciously poor decision.

125. Subcontractors are used whenever cost-effective.

As many of our clients have said, "My biggest challenge is dealing with my employees." As we have said, employees are typically the biggest cost of a business and the greatest potential for liability. People are what make a business work but they don't necessarily have to be employees.

Whenever cost-effective, managers should subcontract work to outside vendors. We do not advocate calling your employees contract laborers to avoid paying payroll taxes. We do suggest, however, using legitimate outside contract labor when it is more cost-effective, when you do not have the needed expertise, or when it reduces the company's risk on the job.

126. Capital expenditures are prioritized.

Capital expenditures are the purchases of equipment, machinery, and vehicles that are normally put on the balance sheet and depreciated. There always seems to be more need for capital expenditures than there is money. Therefore, management must prioritize its capital expenditures.

Obviously capital expenditures required by law must be first. These would include expensive safety and pollution control equipment. The next most important category would be payout projects with the shortest payback period. Payout projects are those that make the company more efficient and, thereby, pay for themselves. Robotics, conveyor systems, and fuel-efficient vehicles would be payout type projects. Finally, the projects that would be useful but don't have a definable pay-out, such as building a new office, should be considered.

127. Management negotiates to reduce costs.

One of the most important skills needed in business is the ability to negotiate. With good negotiating skills and a desire to achieve a win/win situation, management can usually find ways to reduce operating costs and still be fair to vendors. A willingness to negotiate and compromise is the cheapest solution to most business problems.

We got a call from a client who was negotiating with a government agency. The agency had decided to increase the rent by 107 percent on property that our client rented from them. The agency also determined that the insurance coverage was too low. The new insurance requirement would increase our client's premium by 150 percent. He was sick about what these increased costs would do to his business but he wasn't sure what he could do. We encouraged him to negotiate.

The client asked us to analyze the rent increase and he had his insurance agent do the same for the insurance. We then scheduled a meeting with the government agency. We explained to them why the increases were not reasonable or feasible. When the dust settled, there was no increase in the insurance required and less than a 20 percent increase in the rent, which would be locked in for three more years. The ability to negotiate in good faith with reasonable people saved our client thousands of dollars.

128. Reasonable forecasts are used as a basis for budgets.

Overly optimistic sales forecasts are far more common than realistic ones. Ask any banker. Management must determine what is likely to happen when forecasting sales. Inaccurate forecasts can leave the company unprepared for the demand for its products. More commonly, inaccurate forecasts cause the company to spend money on inventory and other expenses in anticipation of sales that never come. If budgets are to be useful, management must do its best to ensure that the forecast is reasonable.

129. Budgets are used to monitor sales and expenditures.

Budgets are indispensable for proper business management. Budgets are a waste of time if they are not used. Every month, the actual sales and expenditures of the company should be compared to the budget. If the budgeted numbers are consistently inconsistent with reality, then the budget should be modified so that future decisions can be made from a more accurate source.

At least once a month we get a call from a new charity soliciting donations. It is our practice to contribute to charities but only according to our budget. These callers are pleasantly but quickly dismissed with the phrase "I'm sorry but that is not in our annual budget. Please send us your literature so we can consider contributing next year."

130. Budgets are used to project cash flow and debt service.

Budgets are typically used to project the profitability of the company. A positive cash flow may not indicate that a business is profitable, but it is essential to determine the success of a business. The budgets should include cash flow adjustments such as inventory or accounts receivable changes, depreciation, and the principal portion of debt service. Only then will management know if the cash flow can keep pace with the cash needs of the business.

131. Purchase discounts are taken if the annualized rate exceeds the borrowing rate.

Purchase discounts should almost always be taken, even if the business has to borrow money to do it. The typical "2 percent 10 days, Net 30" discount represents an annual rate of 36.5 percent. We don't know of any investment that yields such a high return.

The annualized rate is calculated like this. The "2 percent 10 days, Net 30" discount gives you twenty extra days to pay the bill. There are 365 days in a year. So to annualize, you divide the 365 by the 20 extra days. Then you multiply that number times the discount of 2 percent that you get for paying 20 days early. The equation then is $365 \div 20 \times .02 = .365$, which is 36.5 percent.

132. Management is committed to a drug-free workplace.

Most employers we know have this drug policy: If you show up for work drunk or on drugs, you're fired. While we believe that every employee has the right to work in a drug-free workplace, we are not convinced that just firing people who get caught is the wisest policy.

The U.S. Department of Labor funded a study by the Corporation Against Drug Abuse. This study found that up to 25 percent of employees have substance abuse problems. The abuse includes prescription drugs, alcohol, heroin, and marijuana. The study also found that those who use drugs are:

1. Absent from work ten times as many days as nonusers,
2. Over three times more likely to injure themselves or another person in the workplace,
3. Five times more likely to file a workers' compensation claim,
4. One-third less productive, and
5. Often temperamental, causing stress in coworkers and supervisors.

Considering these statistics, employers cannot afford to ignore the problem. Management must do the following:

1. Establish a drug-free workplace policy.
2. Educate employees about the dangers of alcohol and drug abuse.
3. Require drug screening for new employees and for those involved in any type of accident.
4. Help those who need treatment to get it.
5. Terminate employees who will not get or respond to treatment.

133. Management knows that the only thing that is constant is change.

Except for maintaining the core values of integrity and service, those who expect to do business the same way that Grandpa did are destined for failure. In fact, in this ever changing world, to continue to do business the way it was done last year can be a fatal mistake.

Someone ran into the back of Roger's car as they were exiting the freeway. Roger took his car to a local body shop to be repaired. It so happens that this body shop has been in business for more than one hundred years. How could this business have been around a hundred years ago when there weren't any automobiles back then? One hundred years ago they were a blacksmith shop. Times changed, they changed.

Change happens. It will continue to happen and it will happen more rapidly because of technology. Our advice to management: deal with it.

Be positive. Treat people well, including yourself. Watch your costs. Make a profit. Adapt. Management Power Tools will help you achieve a higher level of success.

Management

Item	Score	Weight	Power Tool
76		1	Management directs the business in a positive manner.
77		3	Management is dedicated to long-term profitability.
78		3	Management's integrity is beyond reproach.
79		2	Management is goal oriented.
80		2	The company has a logical organization.
81		2	The company has written standards and objectives.
82		3	Responsibility is delegated to the lowest level possible.
83		2	Delegated authority is not superseded without absolute need.
84		2	Management support of supervisors is apparent to all.

Item	Score	Weight	Power Tool
85		2	The company has regular management meetings.
86		2	The company has regular staff meetings.
87		2	All suggestions are noted and carefully considered.
88		1	Ideas are acted on quickly.
89		2	"Trials" are not held to place blame for mistakes.
90		1	Managers "wander around" to keep in touch with employees.
91		2	Management expects good performance.
92		2	Staffing levels are reviewed regularly.
93		2	There is little excess personnel capacity.
94		2	Overtime is planned and controlled.
95		3	Decreases in staffing levels are handled fairly and with extreme care.
96		1	Excess files, computer programs, procedures, etc. are identified and eliminated.
97		1	The company is not a victim of "paralysis through analysis."
98		1	The company makes a reasonable number of mistakes.
99		2	Customers are billed immediately after delivery.
100		3	Managers take care of their personal lives.
101		2	Profit margins are sufficient for each product.
102		1	Profit margins are tracked monthly.
103		3	Net margins exceed alternate investment yields.

Item	Score	Weight	Power Tool
104		2	Major costs are identified.
105		2	Cost-cutting efforts concentrate on major costs.
106		3	Any change is reviewed for cost/benefit relationship.
107		2	Reducing costs is an ongoing effort.
108		2	No area is exempt from cost-cutting review.
109		2	Financial trends are examined monthly.
110		2	Any change in financial trends is examined in detail.
111		2	Large variances in any account are explained.
112		3	Cash flow is analyzed monthly.
113		1	Cash flow is monitored daily.
114		1	Inventory levels are analyzed for trends.
115		1	Obsolete inventory is identified for liquidation.
116		2	Inventory is purchased according to a plan.
117		2	Cash flow will support the inventory plan.
118		2	Carrying/handling costs do not exceed profit margins.
119		1	Inventory is ordered for just-in-time delivery.
120		2	Purchase orders are issued only by authorized employees.
121		1	Purchasing is independent of operations and accounts payable.
122		2	Goods are approved as they are received.

Item	Score	Weight	Power Tool
123		1	The purchase order is matched to the receiving report and invoice.
124		2	Competitive bids are obtained on all large purchases.
125		1	Subcontractors are used whenever cost-effective.
126		2	Capital expenditures are prioritized.
127		2	Management negotiates to reduce costs.
128		2	Reasonable forecasts are used as a basis for budgets.
129		3	Budgets are used to monitor sales and expenditures.
130		2	Budgets are used to project cash flow and debt service.
131		1	Purchase discounts are taken if the annualized rate exceeds the borrowing rate.
132		2	Management is committed to a drug-free workplace.
133		2	Management knows that the only thing that is constant is change.

4

Accounting: Crunching the Numbers

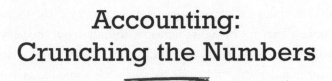

Our firm presented an accounting seminar through the local small business development center. One of the participants stated that after attending the seminar he still couldn't understand how to do accounting. What a revelation! If Roger could have learned how to do accounting in a six-hour seminar, he could have avoided years of schooling, passing the CPA exam, and more years of practical experience.

We often receive in the mail or see in the newspaper an advertisement that promises to make us experts in some area if we will just attend a seminar. Well, we've attended many of those seminars, so why don't we feel like experts? For the same reason that you can't become a marathon racer after a jog around the block. No one can develop expertise in an area unless they *pay the price* by investing the requisite time and effort.

Accounting is a skill that takes time and experience to develop. That does not mean, however, that you cannot produce quality financial information if you don't have a CPA certificate. The following Power Tools will help you determine whether your accounting system is adequate to meet your needs.

134. Monthly financial statements are prepared.

Roger's friend purchased an existing business. The friend was an engineer who enjoyed marketing and who had also passed the CPA exam. One would think that he had all the right skills to run a business. The problem was that he spent his time doing what he enjoyed doing and not doing the books. Three years later, when Roger helped him generate financial statements, it was too late to do anything about the fact that his business had lost money from the very beginning. Sadly, Roger helped him liquidate his assets for the benefit of his creditors, and the friend went to work for someone else—with a large debt still to repay.

Monthly financial statements are critical to the success of any business. This historical financial information is needed by management to take advantage of profitable opportunities and to avoid monetary pitfalls.

135. Monthly financial statements are reviewed by management.

The exercise equipment still in the shipping carton won't help anyone get into shape; financial statements that get filed away without management reviewing them are equally useless. Management must use all of the available tools to properly do their job.

A retail store owner came to us for advice because there was never enough money to pay the rent. We asked to see the financial statements in order to determine why he was not making any money. The owner stated that he had not prepared them for several months because he was too busy with all of his other duties. When the financial statements were finally delivered, a month later, it was obvious that the business was not generating enough revenue to cover its operating costs. The operating costs had been cut to the bone and prices could not be raised and remain competitive. The only way to save the business was to increase sales. Had the financial statements been consistently prepared and reviewed, the owner would have known these facts months earlier. This family business failed because the owner failed to review the financial information that would have told him what he needed to do.

136. Monthly financial statements are timely.

Management must make rapid decisions to keep the company ship off the rocks. Timely financial statements help management make timely decisions. Monthly financial statements should be finalized by approximately the fifteenth of the following month.

Many businesses never seem to be able to prepare financial statements on time. The reason is that there is always some bit of information that they are lacking. Accuracy is critical, but financial statements will never be totally accurate. There are too many assumptions and estimations used in preparing them. The standards of the American Institute of Certified Public Accountants require that financial statements are materially correct, that estimates are conservative, and that the statements are consistently prepared. These standards should be followed whenever preparing a financial statement. We recommend that our clients prepare a time line of activities that must be performed in order to meet the deadline for these statements.

137. Monthly financial statements are accurate.

A timely, but inaccurate, financial statement that is relied upon by management can be deadly to a business. Management makes business decisions based on financial data. If only one number in the financial statements is incorrect, it can be disastrous. Remember, when you are losing money on every unit produced, you will not make a profit just by producing more units. If you are losing money and your financial statements do not show it, you could increase capacity right into bankruptcy.

Many of our consulting engagements were the result of the owners being concerned that their in-house financial statements did not represent reality. That uncertainty can prevent the owner from making the bold decisions that are necessary to keep a business profitable and moving forward.

A manufacturing client called to ask our opinion regarding an accounting problem. The client's bonding company questioned the accuracy of the manufacturers's financial statements. Our client's accountant had mistakenly recorded a liability as an asset. We verified the error and determined that it improperly increased net profit by over $200,000. This, in turn, created a tax liability of $100,000 on money that was never earned.

Often the accuracy of the financial statements is a reflection of the competency of the preparer. Just because the bookkeeper can get the bills paid and the receivables collected does not mean that the bookkeeper is qualified to prepare an accurate financial statement. It would be a good investment to have your CPA evaluate the quality of your in-house financial statements. If the financial statements cannot be relied upon, the CPA could help train the bookkeeper or help you find a competent one.

138. Monthly financial statements reflect company operations.

A company that has three different business segments should have financial statements that show the results of operations from each of the segments. One of our clients sold a segment of his business after we prepared segmented financial statements. He could see that his assets would be more profitably invested in another of his business segments. Separate profit-and-loss statements for major product categories can also be very helpful for the same reason.

139. Cash accounts are reconciled regularly.

Cash has a nasty way of disappearing if there is no accountability. All cash accounts, including petty cash, should be counted and reconciled to the accounting records at least monthly. For example, a petty cash account of $100 should contain a total of $100 in either cash or receipts. Of course, larger cash accounts, including those for retail stores and banks, must be accounted for on a daily basis.

140. All accounts are shown on the general ledger.

Slush funds and "off balance sheet" accounts are not appropriate for businesses. The IRS frowns on this practice also because it distorts the true financial picture. All accounts that are business related should be shown in the general ledger.

141. Unreconciled items are resolved.

When reconciling the general ledger, it is not appropriate to leave account balances unreconciled and give them a fancy name such as "Other." An unreconciled balance is a dollar amount that has no supporting documentation. For example, the ledger shows that the prepaid expense account contains $300, but there is no check or other document that demonstrates payment.

All account balances should be reconciled each month. If there is no supporting evidence for a number, the amount should be eliminated from the balance sheet. Of course, thorough research of the account is necessary first. Carrying these unreconciled account balances is inefficient and undermines the validity and usefulness of the financial statements.

142. Check signers are appropriate in number and responsibility.

Not everyone in the family should be able to sign company checks. The number of people who are authorized to sign checks needs to be sufficient to get the checks signed on time but not so many that any check can get signed at any time. Those signing checks should be responsible people who know the business well enough to know what should be paid and what should not. Some have made the mistake of allowing employees to be check signers as a way of gratifying the employees' ego or as a demonstration that they are trusted. Neither of these reasons makes good business sense.

143. All money received is deposited daily.

All payments made to the company should be deposited in the checking account for proper accounting treatment. If the boss needs cash for some purpose, a check or a petty cash withdrawal slip should be prepared. Circumventing this system, even if you are the boss, can lead to employee dishonesty, inaccurate accounting, and trouble with the IRS.

Roger served as an expert witness in a lawsuit where the owner of a business had regularly taken large sums of cash from the business for personal use. He was suing his bookkeeper, alleging that she had stolen money from his business. He lost the case because his dishonest practices were widely known by his employees. If the bookkeeper had been stealing from him, he would have never known because there was no control over deposits. By the way, his lawsuit opened the doors for the IRS to examine his unreported income!

144. Management reviews cash receipts and disbursements.

If the business is small enough, the owner should sign every check, after reviewing the supporting documentation. The owner should also look at the bank deposit after it is prepared. Personal review by the owner is the best form of internal accounting control. This is the reason that the spouse of a business owner usually is the bookkeeper. As the business grows, many duties have to be delegated to lower levels of management, but final review and approval of receipts and disbursements should never be left to clerks.

We have noticed that many vendors, such as telephone directories, send notices that look like invoices. This is a deceptive form of selling their service. These invoices are often paid because there is inadequate review of supporting documents.

145. Disbursements are consistently approved for payment.

Someone with authority has to take responsibility for approving the payment of all invoices. This approval should be in writing on the file copy of the invoice being sent to Accounting for payment.

146. Disbursements are made only with adequate supporting documentation.

Practically all of the thefts of cash by employees that we know about happened because management did not adequately review supporting documentation when signing checks. We helped a business owner institute better internal control procedures after he discovered that he had paid his bookkeeper several thousand dollars more than their employment agreement required.

In addition, management should review the documentation to ensure that items are received as ordered, that internal control procedures are being followed, and that prices are reasonable. It makes no sense to negotiate price concessions with your vendors and then allow a minimum-wage clerk to pay whatever bill comes in.

Anyone who has been audited by the IRS knows how important it is to have supporting documentation. The IRS will not allow deduction of expenditures that are not supported by adequate documentation. The owner should be as interested as the IRS is in how the money is spent.

147. Checks are signed only after reviewing supporting documents.

Checks should never be signed by anyone unless there is adequate supporting documentation. The supporting documents should bear the initials of the person who verifies that the goods were ordered, were received in good condition, and that the price is correct.

Even if the check appears to be for a legitimate business expense, supporting documentation must be reviewed so that a bill is not paid twice. In our practice, we have seen many clients make duplicate payments on the same invoice. They paid the invoice, then paid again from a copy of the invoice that had been routed elsewhere for a special approval, or from the vendor's statement, on which payment had not yet appeared.

148. Supporting documents are always canceled when paid.

One of the best ways to ensure that an invoice will not be paid twice is to cancel the invoice as it is paid. A "PAID" stamp or other standardized indication on the face of the invoice is sufficient.

149. Disbursements are consistently posted to the proper accounts.

It is important that there is a consistent and logical way of coding the correct general ledger account numbers on disbursements. Inaccurate coding of disbursements renders the financial statements inaccurate, if not useless. For example, if you purchased a new bulldozer and your clerk coded the purchase as office supplies, the profit on your financial statements for that month would be pitiful because bulldozers are depreciated over many years and office supplies are deducted from income as they are purchased. Besides, a bulldozer is not an office supply.

150. Accounts payable are posted and disbursements are made on time.

Accounts payable have to be posted on time if the financial statements are to be accurate. The company that does not post its accounts payable and make disbursements on time usually ends up with a lot of irate phone calls, a bad reputation, and higher prices from the vendors.

Having worked with bankrupt companies, we have a lot of experience dealing with vendors threatening to withdraw credit privileges. At one company, we had to express-mail checks to the supplier to keep the production line working. The calls to the supplier and the hassle of special check handling were essential to the business, but this activity kept us from more productive tasks.

151. Accounts receivable subsidiary ledger totals agree with the general ledger.

An accounts receivable subsidiary ledger lists the amount that each customer owes the company. If the accounts receivable on the general ledger shows a different amount than the subsidiary ledger, there is a big problem. This could mean a reduction in the profit shown on the income statement or it could mean that the person handling accounts receivable is trying to hide incompetence or theft.

A typical scam is to reduce the accounts receivable subsidiary ledger balances but not the accounts receivable general ledger balance when payments are made. The accountant/thief then pockets the payment. The customers don't know that there is a problem because their individual accounts are correct. The owner of the business doesn't know either unless the total of the subsidiary ledgers is compared to the general ledger.

152.   Statements of accounts are mailed monthly.

Mailing monthly statements to customers has a cost. But this cost is generally less than the benefit of reminding customers of what is owed and helping them to understand that you still expect to be paid in full. Good customers will pay their bills but sometimes invoices are lost or temporarily misplaced. A monthly statement notifies the customer of all outstanding invoices so they can be found and paid. Helping customers to pay on time will also prevent potential conflicts between your employees who are selling and your employees who are collecting.

We like to send messenges to our customers' clients when we are helping with collections. A handwritten note on the face of the statement has produced great results. These messages range from "Why aren't you paying your bill?" to "See you in court."

153.   All customers are on the aged accounts receivable.

Customers should pay according to your payment terms. Some will not. Creating an aged accounts receivable listing is the best way to separate the good customers from the potential deadbeats. This list is the basis for collection efforts.

A typical aging will separate the amounts due in columns for the following: total amount due, current amount due, 30 days past due, 60 days past due, and 90+ days past due. The intensity of collection efforts will increase as the amount due from the customer moves from one column to the next.

154.   All accounts are aged accurately.

The accounts receivable must be aged correctly in order to know what type of action needs to be taken with a customer. An accurate aging can prevent embarrassing mistakes, such as turning a good customer over for collection or allowing a deadbeat customer to continue to buy when they never pay the bill.

155. Profit margins are determinable.

The major reason for preparing financial statements is to determine whether the business is making money. The accounting system of any business should be able to show the profit margin on sales before general and administrative costs.

156. Periodic physical inventories are consistently taken.

A physical inventory means actually counting and determining the cost of the inventory that is owned by the company. Physical inventories are absolutely essential to validate the ending inventory and the cost of sales that is calculated by the accounting system. Relying on what is shown on the books and ignoring the inventory that is actually on hand is ignoring reality. Inaccuracies in inventory can make a company that is losing money look like it is very profitable. A client of ours has seen changes of over $100,000 in net income because the book inventory had to be adjusted to agree with the physical inventory.

157. Book inventories are reconciled to physical inventories.

Once a physical inventory has been taken, the inventory on your accounting system or book inventory should be adjusted to reflect the results of the physical inventory. Large variances between the physical and the book inventories need to be investigated. Sometimes the units of measure used by the accounting system and the physical inventory counter are different. For example, quantities counted in pounds could be kept on the accounting system in tons. So a physical count of five pounds could be incorrectly shown in the accounting system as ten thousand pounds.

158. Inventory reconciliation is immediately performed.

Reconciliation of the book and the physical inventories should be immediately performed so that variances can be investigated before the physical inventory has changed. Individual physical inventory counts can be wrong and it is extremely difficult to reconstruct what was on hand at the end of the month if you wait until the twenty-second of the next month to do it.

159. The physical inventory agrees with the general ledger.

It is important to the accuracy of the financial statements that the inventory shown on the general ledger agrees with the physical inventory. The accounting system inventory tracks what should be happening, but the physical inventory shows *what is happening*.

160. Inventories are valued at the lower of cost or market value.

The value assigned to inventory can have a tremendous effect on the financial statements. Generally accepted accounting principles require that inventories be valued at the lower of the initial cost or the current market value of the inventory. In this way, the financial statements will accurately reflect losses when the market price for the inventory has decreased. For example, if you were to buy barley at $100 per ton and the market value decreased to $60 per ton, the barley should be valued at $60 per ton. If not, the inventory would be valued at more than the potential selling price. Not devaluing the inventory, when you know that the value has decreased, just delays the recognition of the eventual loss that will result.

161. The capitalization policy is followed.

A policy should be in place that defines which purchases are an expense to the company and which are fixed assets that will be depreciated over time. The IRS has a definite interest in this decision because it can dramatically affect current net income. There are separate guidelines for tax and financial reporting purposes. Generally, a fixed asset is one that has a life of more than one year and a price of over $500.

162. The fixed asset ledger is maintained.

An accurate listing of all fixed assets is important. It is necessary for income tax purposes and, generally, for property tax purposes. After paying all those taxes, it's nice to keep a list of what you own so it doesn't get lost. This will be particularly important if the business is ever listed for sale or if a business valuation needs to be done.

163. Fixed assets are properly set up and depreciated.

Fixed assets are included on the fixed asset ledger as they are purchased. The important facts to record are a description of the asset, an identifying number, the purchase price and date, the useful life, and the scrap value and the depreciation methods for book, federal, and state tax purposes. A good fixed asset accounting system can help reduce the taxable income of the company, save personnel time, and reduce tax preparation fees.

164. Fixed assets are properly retired.

Removing fixed assets from the fixed asset ledger can save the company money. Property taxes are generally assessed on all assets, even if they are fully depreciated. Property and auto insurance costs are also generally determined by which assets are on the fixed asset ledger. One of our bankruptcy clients had so many old, junk vehicles that the company didn't know what was registered and insured and what wasn't.

165.   Fixed asset inventories are taken.

A fixed asset inventory can be taken whenever it seems prudent to do so. This inventory verifies that the assets listed on the fixed asset ledger are still there. We performed a fixed asset inventory for a client and removed two dozen vehicles from the property tax and insurance list, saving the company thousands of dollars.

166.   The balance sheet is in balance.

It sounds self-evident, but balance sheets must balance. This means that the total assets should equal the sum of the liabilities and owner's equity. Assets (A) are the things the business owns, liabilities (L) are what the business owes, and owner's equity (OE) is the difference ($A = L + OE$). A balance sheet that does not balance could be an indication of an inaccurate accounting system and an income statement that is meaningless.

167.   Income shown on the income statement equals the increase in equity on the balance sheet.

This is a quick way to impress your accounting friends. Look at the equity section of your balance sheet and verify that the increase or decrease in equity since the last financial statement is equal to the income or loss shown on the income statement. If it isn't, your accounting is inaccurate.

168.   The income statement reflects only actual income.

Before we began working with one of our clients, he had sent financial statements to the bank that showed his equipment at his estimate of market value. He was trying to renegotiate his line of credit but he was unsuccessful. The owner then hired us and Roger called the banker to inform him of our engagement. The banker said that the bank would not consider working with the client until the financial statements showed the equipment at its purchase price, as generally accepted accounting principles require. The corrections were made and the negotiations with the bank were successful.

Some business owners like to show how much their company is worth by inflating the cost of their assets to market value or showing sales that have been negotiated but not consummated. This has the effect of overstating income and equity. It is a sign of ignorance at best and fraud at worst. Artificially inflating income destroys one's credibility with bankers, bonding companies, and stockholders.

169.   The income statement is sufficiently detailed.

Financial statements are to be used. They can only be used if they are sufficiently detailed to be meaningful to the user. Many audited financial statements show only major categories of revenue and expense. This is adequate for financial reporting but it is not adequate for management purposes. The income statement must show detailed account balances in order for management to do the analysis that is necessary for proper management decisions.

170.   Account titles are accurate and specific.

The titles on general ledger accounts should reflect the purposes of the accounts. Specific accounts need to be established to capture important costs for analysis. For example, instead of an account titled Sales Expense, the sales expenses should be broken down into Advertising Expenses, Customer Meals and Entertainment, Sales Travel, and Dues and Subscriptions. Avoid the "Miscellaneous" account whenever possible.

171. Prepaid accounts are adjusted to actual amounts.

A prepaid account is established for payments made in advance of the delivery of goods or services. The most typical use of this account is for prepaid insurance coverage. It is important for the accuracy of the income statement to remove the prepayment from the account as the insurance, or other goods or service, has been used or expired.

172. The type of business organization is correct.

Whether a business operates as a C-corporation, S-corporation, sole proprietorship, partnership, or a limited liability company should be a conscious decision. Each of these business types has its own unique advantages and disadvantages. Business owners should choose the correct type of business organization after consultation with their attorney and CPA. Then this issue should be reviewed regularly to examine whether conditions have changed enough to justify a change in business type.

173. Detailed records are maintained on all active accounts.

Good accounting records include having the detail that supports the balance in each balance sheet account. This is particularly true of bank accounts, inventories, accounts payable, and accounts receivable. These accounts typically have a large volume of transactions, and account variances have an immediate effect on the profitability of the company.

174. Equity and draw accounts are reconciled monthly.

It is important to carefully monitor the equity section of the balance sheet. This is critical if the owner is taking draws from the company. A draw is money that a partner or sole proprietor receives from the business instead of a regular paycheck. Errors in this account can have significant tax consequences because draws are not a deductible expense to the company. If a legitimate expense were to be coded as a draw, then the owner would have to pay income tax that was not really owed.

175. Suspense accounts are eliminated.

"If you don't know what it is, put it in Suspense." This seems to be the motto of marginal accountants. All transactions should be described as well as possible, coded so as not to overstate income, and then tracked until they can be definitely classified. Suspense accounts on formal financial statements are totally unacceptable.

176. Financial statements are prepared according to generally accepted accounting principles.

Creative accounting methods are more prevalent in small businesses that do not have formal audits, but all financial statements should be prepared according to generally accepted accounting principles (GAAP). Bankers and well informed shareholders expect GAAP to be used. GAAP helps to insure that financial information is consistent, conservative, and comparable with other companies. It has been our experience that a bank will not loan money to a business if they do not have properly prepared financial statements or tax returns.

177.   Financial records are kept using the double-entry system.

The double-entry system is the one that records a debit and a credit for each financial transaction. Most accounting software uses this system automatically. Although it was first introduced way back in 1494 by Fra Luca Pacioli, a Franciscan monk, no one has come up with a better way to do accounting than the double-entry system that accountants still use today. Use it. It works!

178.   The accrual method is always used for management reports.

The accrual method in its simplest form means that you record income when it is earned rather than when it is collected, and you record liabilities when they are incurred rather than when they are paid. People joke about keeping two sets of books but it is legitimate. If you meet the IRS requirements, you can have your tax return prepared using the cash method of accounting and your management reports prepared using the accrual method. But beware, the accrual method is the only way you can truly gauge whether you are making money from month to month.

Using the cash method of accounting, you could show a wonderful profit by not paying any bills for that month! On the other hand, if your customer takes thirty days to pay a large invoice, you could show a huge loss and think that the business is a failure. Neither of these scenarios represent reality. Sales and expenses must be recognized when they are incurred rather than when money is exchanged.

179. Personal and business expenses are never commingled.

Personal expenses should not be paid out of the business, period. It is important that personal and business expenses be kept separate to preserve the accuracy of personal and company tax returns, to determine whether the business is making money, and to ensure that all family employees and owners are compensated fairly. Just because yours is a family business does not mean that you can pay your home mortgage from the company till. It is illegal to do so and it is foolish.

Roger was appointed as a receiver of a business owned by a father and his son. The father filed suit against the son when he learned that the son was using company checks to buy groceries and pay other personal expenses. Aside from the fact that commingling personal and business expenses is illegal and unethical, it creates serious family conflicts too.

180. Adequate records are kept for IRS requirements.

The Internal Revenue Service has special rules for different kinds of expenses such as travel, entertainment, personal auto use, and contributions. These rules must be followed in order to file an accurate tax return. Ask the person who prepares your tax return how to accumulate the needed information throughout the year. Separate expense accounts must be established in order for the accounting system to do most of the work in gathering this data.

181. Payments on account are matched to invoices.

As payments are received, they should be matched to the invoice to which they apply. If the customer does not pay by invoice, the next best thing to do is to apply the payments to the oldest balance on the customer's accounts receivable ledger. If there is a finance charge on the customer's account, apply the payment to the finance charge first.

182. Allowance for doubtful accounts is reasonable.

Very few businesses collect on every sale on account they make. Financial statements have to be accurate to be beneficial; therefore, a realistic allowance for accounts that will not be collected is essential. This allowance for doubtful accounts should be prepared by analyzing all of the past due accounts and then assigning an overall percentage of noncollectability for each account that is past due. "Allowance for doubtful accounts" is accounting terminology. It does not imply that you should abandon collection efforts. Even though a customer is part of the allowance for doubtful accounts, you still must aggressively pursue all past due amounts until they are collected or are determined to be uncollectible.

183. Credits to accounts are properly approved.

Only authorized people should have the authority to approve credit memos to customers' accounts receivable. Credit memos are powerful; they reduce your bottom line. This important internal control feature will protect income by preventing employee theft and errors.

One of our clients had a manager that credited customers' accounts so often that they began to expect it. This practice resulted in accounts receivable not being collected until credits were given, both deserved and undeserved. The undeserved credits thus decreased net income for no valid reason.

Utilize generally accepted accounting principles. Be accurate. Be timely. Analyze your financial statements. Don't cheat. Accounting may seem boring but these Power Tools tell you if you're making money.

Accounting

Item	Score	Weight	Power Tool
134		3	Monthly financial statements are prepared.
135		3	Monthly financial statements are reviewed by management.
136		2	Monthly financial statements are timely.
137		3	Monthly financial statements are accurate.
138		2	Monthly financial statements reflect company operations.
139		2	Cash accounts are reconciled regularly.
140		1	All accounts are shown on the general ledger.
141		1	Unreconciled items are resolved.
142		2	Check signers are appropriate in number and responsibility.
143		3	All money received is deposited daily.
144		3	Management reviews cash receipts and disbursements.
145		1	Disbursements are consistently approved for payment.
146		3	Disbursements are made only with adequate supporting documentation.
147		3	Checks are signed only after reviewing supporting documents.
148		1	Supporting documents are always canceled when paid.
149		2	Disbursements are consistently posted to the proper accounts.
150		2	Accounts payable are posted and disbursements are made on time.

Item	Score	Weight	Power Tool
151		2	Accounts receivable subsidiary ledger totals agree with the general ledger.
152		1	Statements of accounts are mailed monthly.
153		2	All customers are on the aged accounts receivable.
154		2	All accounts are aged accurately.
155		2	Profit margins are determinable.
156		2	Periodic physical inventories are consistently taken.
157		2	Book inventories are reconciled to physical inventories.
158		1	Inventory reconciliation is immediately performed.
159		2	The physical inventory agrees with the general ledger.
160		1	Inventories are valued at the lower of cost or market value.
161		2	The capitalization policy is followed.
162		1	The fixed asset ledger is maintained.
163		2	Fixed assets are properly set up and depreciated.
164		1	Fixed assets are properly retired.
165		1	Fixed asset inventories are taken.
166		2	The balance sheet is in balance.
167		2	Income shown on the income statement equals the increase in equity on the balance sheet.
168		3	The income statement reflects only actual income.

Item	Score	Weight	Power Tool
169		2	The income statement is sufficiently detailed.
170		1	Account titles are accurate and specific.
171		2	Prepaid accounts are adjusted to actual amounts.
172		3	The type of business organization is correct.
173		2	Detailed records are maintained on all active accounts.
174		2	Equity and Draw accounts are reconciled monthly.
175		1	Suspense accounts are eliminated.
176		3	Financial statements are prepared according to generally accepted accounting principles.
177		2	Financial records are kept using the double-entry system.
178		2	The accrual method is always used for management reports.
179		3	Personal and business expenses are never commingled.
180		2	Adequate records are kept for IRS requirements
181		1	Payments on account are matched to invoices.
182		1	Allowance for doubtful accounts is reasonable.
183		2	Credits to accounts are properly approved.

5

Protection:
Keeping It All in the Family

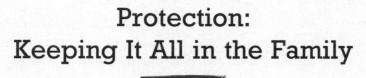

It was shaping up as a good year for our client. In fact, it was the company's best year ever. Sales were increasing dramatically and net income was the stuff of which dreams are made. That was when the nightmares began.

The computer hard drive that contained all the contract and accounting data, including millions of dollars in accounts receivable, crashed. Our client tried to restore from the mirror drive, which was designed for this type of problem, but the company's computer consultant had turned off the mirror drive because he thought that it was causing system errors. They tried to restore from the tape drive, but it did not work either because dust had corrupted the mechanism. The data was eventually all recovered by sending the hard drive to a recovery service.

After hundreds of employee hours to bring the system current, things were just starting to get back to normal in the office. Then, the business owner's worst nightmare struck. A company delivery truck hit a school bus full of kids. There were no fatalities, but one child was seriously injured. The total cost of this accident still has not been determined.

These two nightmares could have easily destroyed the dream year. They did not because proper protection Power Tools were in place. There was a modest impact on current income, and insurance premiums will be higher in subsequent years. These costs will be relatively inconsequential because the owners had wisely protected the business.

The following protection Power Tools will help you chase away many of your business nightmares. You can then concentrate on making more money—and you will sleep a lot better!

184. Liability insurance is adequate to protect equity.

When you buy insurance, you are essentially betting that something awful is going to happen to your business, and the insurance company is betting that it won't. Certainly, we hope that the insurance company is right!

Liability insurance coverage should, at a minimum, equal the equity you have in your business. Buying insurance is a good way to protect the business for you and your family.

185. Insurance is adequate to prevent personal liability.

Liability insurance coverage should be sufficient to show a jury that you were being conscientious in protecting the public, especially if the equity in your business is small. Legal precedent has shown that owners of corporations with very little liability insurance have been held personally liable for damage awards.

186. Management is aware of insurance coverage.

The time to determine what kind of insurance was in place is not after the warehouse burns down. Management should be involved in the insurance purchasing process enough to know what has been covered and its related cost.

187. Coverage has been removed from retired assets.

A process should be in place and a person designated to remove coverage from retired assets. There is no reason to pay for something that you are not getting. It is equally important that coverage be added when assets are purchased or placed in service. For example, we removed eighteen retired vehicles from the policy of a client, saving hundreds of dollars annually.

188. Limits of coverage are reviewed annually.

Things change and assets generally lose value over time. These are two good reasons to reevaluate insurance coverage. For example, a company that insures a building for $1 million even though it is worth only $500,000 is wasting money. If the building were destroyed, the insurance company, except in rare circumstances, would only pay for the true value of the building.

189. Competitive bids are obtained on insurance.

The insurance industry, like most industries, goes through cycles. Individual carriers will raise or lower their rates in response to what is happening in their industry as well as what is happening in their company. Therefore, to never consider another insurance carrier can be a costly decision. It is prudent for the business to get competitive bids on insurance every year. It is also beneficial to have other insurance brokers bid on your insurance every other year. This practice will keep everyone honest.

190.   Health insurance coverage is competitive.

You may choose to bid your health insurance less frequently than liability insurance because of potential problems with preexisting medical conditions, changes in care providers, and continuity of coverage and rates. However, one of the most alarming cost increases of the eighties was medical costs. It is important to control these costs by every means available, including getting competitive bids on health insurance coverage, changing deductible amounts, or instituting a pretax, employee insurance copay.

191.   Key person life insurance coverage is in place.

Most small- to medium-sized businesses are built around the genius of the founder. It is important to the continuity and value of the business to insure the life of that key person. Key person life insurance will give the business the money it needs during the transition from the founder to new management, or it will give the owners time to sell the business for the highest price.

192.   Deductible limits are at the most cost-effective levels.

Deductible limits are an indication of how much risk the company is willing to accept. The higher the deductible limit, the more risk the company accepts and vice versa. For this reason, deductibles have a direct impact on insurance premiums. Deductible limits can be set too high or too low depending on how much risk the company can assume.

It would be foolish to set automobile deductible limits at $50 per occurrence on a fleet of autos and rolling stock. A low deductible could drive the premium up to where the cost exceeds the benefit.

Therefore, it is important that management determines the deductible limits rather than leaving this task to the insurance agent.

193. Workers' compensation claims are monitored.

A company whose workers' compensation costs are significantly higher than the competition's will have a difficult time competing. Workers' compensation costs for many companies can be the difference between being profitable and not.

Workers' compensation abuse has been rather common in the past. Some cases that seem outrageous have been documented on TV investigative reporting shows. When insurance companies started to aggressively pursue workers' compensation abuse legislation and workers' compensation abusers, the number of claims decreased significantly.

We helped one client save over $80,000 in one year in workers' compensation costs by instituting a safety committee and letting the insurance company know that we were monitoring the claims. The committee met regularly to discuss outstanding claims and ways to prevent similar claims in the future. A claims specialist from the insurance company met with the committee quarterly to discuss the status of claims and to share information. If your insurance company is not aggressively pursuing claims, notify them of your concerns and then begin searching for a better insurance company.

194. Claims are processed quickly.

The more quickly claims are processed, the less costly they will be to the company. This is because the information necessary to protect the company will be more readily available. The workers' compensation insurance law in many states requires that injuries be reported to the carrier within twenty-four hours of the occurrence. One person in the company should have the responsibility of filing and following up on claims to ensure promptness and consistency.

195. Injured workers are encouraged to return to work ASAP.

It is not healthy for the company or the injured employee to stay at home any longer than is required by a doctor. Wise company management will modify job duties so the employee can get back to work instead of getting comfortable staying at home and getting paid for it.

There is a reason that personal injury attorneys advertise heavily on afternoon TV soap operas. There seems to be some magical correlation between how many lawyer ads an injured employee sees and how severe the injury becomes. In summary, when employees stay home longer than necessary, workers' compensation costs go up, legal actions begin, and employees seem to lose interest in going back to work.

196. Minor accidents are settled with a liability release.

Sometimes property damage accidents are so minor that the company will just pay the owner of the property for the damage. When this is done, the company should get a liability release from the owner of the property in exchange for the damage payment. The insurance agent will help in this process.

197. Inventories are physically protected from damage or theft.

In many companies, inventories represent a major investment. This investment, like any other, should be adequately protected from the elements and from theft. Alarms, fencing, sprinklers, improved night lighting, and security services should all be considered.

198. Security over fixed assets is adequate.

At least the same protection that is given to inventories is appropriate for the company's fixed assets, including machinery, automobiles, and computers. A safety coordinator could be designated by management to oversee the security of all assets.

We have had clients who kept dogs on the premises for security. When visiting one facility, we would park as close to the office as possible, carefully check to see if the dog was near, and then make a mad dash to the office door before the dog caught the scent of fear. This dog made the Employee of the Month parking place an especially valued reward. Consider if the dog is a greater liability to the company than the theft that could occur.

199. Legal counsel is competent and independent.

Just because your brother-in-law, Landon the legal eagle, is an attorney doesn't mean that he should be the company's legal counsel. Landon must pass two tests. First, he must be competent. Second, he must have independent opinions and not just those given to him by his spouse, who happens to be your sister.

The attorney's competency and independence can both be proven in battle. If your attorney fails to show these qualities in the first few legal actions, start looking for a new attorney. Family members can serve both competently and independently as counsel to the company.

200. Legal counsel is consulted on all legal issues.

The most common complaint that we hear from attorneys is "Why didn't my client come to me sooner?" It is not set in stone that you consult with an attorney only if you are in serious trouble. We know business owners who don't want to pay for legal advice because they think they can get by without it. Your attorney should give advice that will help your business avoid problems. As Dad used to say, "It doesn't do any good to close the barn door after the horse is already gone." So take a lesson from smart equestrians: call your attorney if you have any doubt. Better yet, take your attorney to lunch regularly. It is amazing how much information you can get for the price of a taco.

Attorneys are the butt of thousands of great jokes. Our experience has been, however, that most attorneys are good folks. We take our own advice and spend a lot of social time with attorneys learning all we can, and telling them the latest attorney jokes.

201.   A competent tax preparer prepares the tax return.

You know that just about anyone can prepare a tax return. It won't necessarily be correct, but anyone can prepare one. It does not make a lot of sense to pay your daughter, the recent college graduate, $50 to prepare your business tax return when the IRS can assess you thousands of dollars in penalties and interest for a faulty return. A competent CPA not only will prepare a reliable tax return but can also help with legitimate tax strategies to build an estate that is worthy of being passed on to the kids. An enrolled agent, who is licensed to practice before the IRS tax court, is also qualified to prepare a tax return.

Even though Roger is a CPA, he does not prepare tax returns, because he does not keep current with changes in the IRS code. He employs a CPA that specializes in taxation to prepare his client's tax returns. We have seen tax returns prepared by unqualified people that if audited by even the most novice IRS agents would have cost thousands of dollars in penalties and interest.

202. Correspondence from governmental agencies is handled immediately.

We know a business owner who would throw any envelope with an IRS return address into a box to be given to the CPA when the tax returns were prepared. *Baaaaaaad* idea! It doesn't take a genius to figure out that the penalties were huge. Anything that comes from a governmental agency should be opened immediately, read, and answered. Even if you can't do what the government wants you to do, some action on your part will keep them from getting nasty. Remember, the government carries a big stick.

203. All tax payments are made on time.

Roger was the trustee for a company that owed the IRS over $1 million in unpaid withholding taxes. This kind of debt is not forgiven in a bankruptcy and becomes the personal liability of the officers of the company.

Many people get caught in the trap of not paying withheld taxes because the IRS and the state don't come after the money immediately. So the owner always says that he will catch up on the taxes when the next money comes in. It comes in and goes out and no payment is made because it will be caught up next time, and so forth. You can owe money to the vendors. You can owe money to your mother-in-law. But, never, never, never owe money to the government.

204. The company fosters a positive working relationship with its bank.

Most businesses are leveraged with money borrowed from a bank. This relationship can help the business grow and expand. It is a healthy relationship as long as the banker is happy. If the banker loses confidence in your business, it can be the beginning of the end. Bankers are not usually excited about picking up a business that was kicked out of some other bank. It is important to satisfy the banker, no matter how petty the requests seem to you. If you see trouble brewing, find another bank *before* you are asked to leave.

205.   The bank is kept informed of the company's operations.

Your banker should be on the list of people you take out to lunch regularly. In this casual atmosphere you can discuss how things are going, ask for advice, and generally make the banker feel comfortable with the loans made to you. The more information that you give to the banker, the more you will be trusted. Bankers make their living by accumulating and monitoring data on your business, so give until they say, "Enough."

206.   The company complies with all terms of its loan agreements.

Loan agreements are legal documents that can be used to beat you into submission. It is foolish to think that the bank will ignore the loan documents and give you what you want. As a bankruptcy trustee, Roger has seen too many people make this mistake. Every one of them lost. If there are terms that are overly burdensome or that just do not make sense anymore, discuss them with the banker and ask that they be modified. Remember this: it is better for you to be mad at your banker than for your banker to be mad at you.

Over the years, we have developed working relationships with bankers who have the job of monitoring and collecting bad loans. These bankers work in a division of the bank that is usually called the Special Assets Department. The S.A.D. acronym is very apropos. Every business in Special Assets is there because it violated its loan agreements. Once you are in this ominous department, it is difficult, though not impossible, to escape. Other banks typically will not finance these businesses because the bankers consider them to be too risky. The S.A.D. businesses usually end up in bankruptcy.

207. Banking, legal, and CPA relationships are changed only after careful consideration.

Business relationships, like any other kind, take time to develop. These relationships should be entered into with the assumption that they will last a long time. They need to be nurtured so that, eventually, you can reap the benefits. People who bounce from one professional to another quickly get a reputation in the community. This can lead the professionals to get all they can while the getting is good. On the other hand, a business that fosters good working relationships with its banker, lawyer, and CPA seems to get a lot of free advice and a flow of very important information, because the parties have come to trust one another.

208. Management seeks and heeds professional advice in all technical disciplines.

Business owners primarily have two problems regarding professional advice: one, they do not want to pay for the help they need; and, two, they get advice from the professional and then ignore it.

Roger has a bad habit of telling his wife, and the mother of their nine children, how to take care of the house and discipline the kids. She says, "Well, aren't you Mr. Everything!" We don't think she means it as a compliment. No one can be an expert in all departments. Buy the help you need and then use it.

209. New employee references are checked.

No matter how well the new employee interviews, call the references. There might be a skeleton in the closet of which you should be aware. Even then you will miss some important information, but you will miss a lot less than if you did not check the references. It would also be a good idea to call the authors of any written recommendations supplied by the applicant.

Roger called the references of a potential employee for one of his clients. He was told that the employee was very good at what he did but sometimes acted strangely. Roger advised the client to hire the employee because all of the employee references were good except for the one comment about his acting strangely. Things went well for several months until the employee showed up for work drunk, with a gun. We now know what "acting strangely" means.

Many companies have a policy to not give any information about the applicant other than the fact that they were employed. Always ask the former employers if they would rehire the applicant. A simple yes or no answer can be very meaningful.

210.   Dishonesty of any kind is not tolerated.

Being honest is like being pregnant: either you are or you aren't. If management overlooks any kind of dishonesty in the employees, the employees will assume that it is not that important. A company where honesty is not important will have employee theft.

Russ was hired to manage a team of salespeople. One of the salespeople warned him that her colleague, Jill, was fudging on her time card. She said the previous manager knew about it, but never did anything. Soon after that, a customer came and purchased $3,000 worth of merchandise. Jill didn't wait on the customer, but she ended up taking the money, literally. When Russ reviewed the day's sales and found that the cash was missing, he asked Jill if she knew anything about it. Jill confessed that she had it at home. She returned the cash, but Russ had to fire her anyway. Small indiscretions can demonstrate large character flaws. Deal with them as they arise to avoid potential problems in the future.

211. An effective safety program is followed.

A safe workplace is an enjoyable and productive workplace. In addition, the company saves money in workers' compensation claims; employee lost time; accident, liability, and workers' compensation insurance premiums; governmental agency fines and penalties; and loss of employee productivity. Safety programs cost money initially but, in the long run, they pay for themselves many times over.

212. The company complies with all governmental safety policies.

A safety supervisor position is important in any size company, even if the safety supervisor is the owner. This person ensures that the company complies with all governmental safety guidelines. Failure to do so could cause the failure of the business because of OSHA fines or closures, and lawsuits.

213. Hazardous working conditions are not tolerated.

Correcting hazardous working conditions can be costly, but there is no acceptable alternative. The death or injury of an employee due to known hazardous working conditions is a sign to everyone that the business owner cares more about the bottom line than about human life. The death or injury of an employee is also very costly to the business in workers' compensation claims, lawsuits, loss of productivity, and OSHA fines. Begin today to correct any hazardous working conditions in your company. Your insurance carrier will be delighted to give you a free safety inspection if you just ask. Remember, the insurer is betting that you won't have any accidents.

Roger walked through a client's workplace with an inspector from the California OSHA. The inspector was there in response to a safety hazard claim made by a former employee. The employee had been fired from his job for absenteeism and he then filed a workers' compensation claim for a back injury. He had jumped from a second-story storage area instead of using the stairs. The inspector was there to verify that the company had installed a railing around the storage area. In his walk-through, the inspector identified five safety violations for which the company would have been fined if he were doing an official safety check. Safe practices will protect your pocketbook as well as your employees.

214. Computer file backup is performed daily.

Computers are marvelous tools but even they can fail. A business can not afford to lose its accounts receivable listing. Therefore, a backup file needs to be created every day because no one knows when or if the system will go down.

215. Computer backup is stored off-site.

A computer backup file won't be very useful if it is destroyed in the same fire that melts the computer. Someone needs to take the backup file home with them or put it in a safe off-site location.

216. An alternate source for data processing is available.

It might never be used, but having an alternate source for processing your data should be in place. If the company's data processing capability is damaged or destroyed, the company must continue to bill customers and pay vendors and employees in order to survive. Make arrangements with another company that has similar data processing equipment to use their system in case of an emergency. Reciprocal arrangements make the most sense. You might have to do all your accounting after midnight but you will still be in business.

217. Data files are password protected.

The military calls it "need to know." Not everyone in your organization needs to know the information that is stored in your computer system. Password protection will allow management to determine who should have access to the accounts receivable files and who should not. Entry into the system and all sensitive files should be password protected.

218. Computer programs are documented, copied, and stored off-site.

If your computer programmer were run over by a truck, could anyone else figure out the computer programs that the company is using? Computer programmers are not famous for documenting their programs or changes to the programs. This bad habit is great job security for the programmer but very expensive for the company if the programmer ever leaves. The cost of a new programmer analyzing computer code can be as high as the cost of buying a completely new software package. Computer programs should also be copied and stored off-site in case of an emergency.

219. Personnel policies are written.

The lack of written personnel policies has been very costly to many businesses. Without a written policy, employees and juries have been left to determine what the policy should have been and how much the business should have to pay for violating it. There are many boilerplate personnel manuals available in written and computer format. These manuals can be a starting point for creating a manual that documents your own personnel policies.

A common question from our clients is "Can I fire this person?"

Our answer is always the same: "What does your personnel manual say and have you consistently followed the procedures?" If the client does not have a personnel manual, he or she suddenly understands the importance of one.

220. Personnel policies are consistently administered.

Personnel policies that are not consistently administered are worse than no policies at all. Treating one employee differently from another is the basis for any discrimination lawsuit. Do not allow the business to violate personnel policies because the person requesting it is your child or your best worker. Even though it might seem justified in your own mind, this will open the door to employee dissatisfaction and potential legal liability for discrimination.

We were contracted by a grand jury to conduct a management audit. We surveyed the employees to determine if there were any problems in the organization. Several of the employees complained that management was inconsistent in handling personnel matters. The inconsistency caused many productive employees to quit. The straw that broke the camel's back was when the department manager's son physically attacked a coworker. The department manager gave him a day off without pay instead of following policy, which dictated termination.

Some employers are so afraid of a wrongful termination lawsuit that they say, "Let's make it so hard on———that he quits." There are two things to remember: one, anyone can sue anyone else, at any time, for any reason; and, two, "making it hard on———" is a great way to increase the punitive damages that a jury will award to the employee when he or she wins a lawsuit.

221. One person coordinates personnel policy administration.

The best way to ensure consistency in personnel policy administration is to have one person designated to coordinate all aspects of human resources. The decisions might not always be correct but they will be fairly consistent. Another benefit is that only one person will have to research personnel problems, instead of all supervisors trying to find answers to very similar questions.

In the process of reorganizing a department, Russ had to transfer a data processor to another building. Russ explained why the move was required and introduced her to her new coworkers. When the day arrived, Russ was shocked when she refused to go. He had never encountered this situation, so he was at a loss for what to do. Fortunately the company had designated one person to handle such problems. The human resources manager had experience with similar situations and outlined the necessary steps to terminate the employee for insubordination.

222. Policies address progressive discipline, discrimination, and harassment.

The personnel manual could have a thousand and one different policies. There are, however, some policies that are absolutely necessary. They are those that deal with discipline, discrimination, and harassment. These are the policies that are the basis for most legal action against companies. It would be advisable to have your legal counsel review your policies in these areas.

223. All personnel complaints are investigated quickly and completely.

The people in your company are your greatest resource. They are also the greatest source of problems. Pay attention to the concerns of employees because they can help you find more profitable ways of doing business, and if you ignore personnel complaints, the results can destroy your company. Investigating and acting quickly on employee complaints will foster goodwill among the employees, reduce tensions, and show a positive pattern if one of them were ever to sue the company.

224.   Everyone's work is subject to review and approval.

Even Laura the bookkeeper, who has been with the company for thirty years, can make mistakes. We know of several companies that were forced into bankruptcy because trusted and loyal employees were stealing from the company coffers. Therefore, *everyone's* work should be subject to review and approval. This is not a matter of questioning someone's integrity. It is simply good business.

225.   All credit is preapproved and routinely reviewed.

The marketing gurus will tell you that there is nothing more important than the sale. But a sale is not complete until the money is collected. Your company needs a well designed credit application that is properly completed and signed by the customer. A credit report should then be ordered. The credit manager reviews both the credit application and the credit report, and makes a decision as to the credit worthiness of the applicant. If the credit manager approves the credit, sales on account can be made to the potential customer. The credit manager should routinely evaluate the paying habits of the customer to determine continued credit worthiness. It's a hassle but it's worth it.

226.   Past due accounts are monitored weekly.

Past due accounts need to be reviewed, and collection calls made, on a weekly basis. More frequent follow-up calls to slow-paying customers are ineffective; less frequent calls allow them to think the pressure is off. It is critical to document each call and customer response on a permanent record. The record of calls is referred to when making the next call to the customer. Instead of saying, "I'm sure that you promised to pay this week," the collector is in a much more powerful position when saying, "My record shows that you promised to pay this invoice on June 5, 12, and 19. You will deliver the check to my office today or we will begin legal action."

227.   Collection procedures are consistent, insistent, and persistent.

Most collections can be done more effectively in-house than by sending them out to collection agencies. In-house collection gives the company more control and can cost a lot less. However, for it to be effective, the credit manager must have the personality to make collection calls. The calls must be consistently made, preferably every week. Demands for payment must be insistent, typically asking for a particular date that the bill will be paid. The credit manager must also be persistent in pursuing the debtor. One client's sales force calls Roger "The Kiss of Death" because they know if their customers do not pay their bills, the only way they'll avoid Roger is to file bankruptcy.

228.   Legal counsel is used to send dunning letters.

A very inexpensive way to get the attention of slow-paying customers is to have your attorney send them a standard dunning letter. This nasty-gram goes out on the attorney's stationery, signed by the attorney. This is inexpensive because the attorney's secretary can complete the standard format with just a couple of items of information from the company: the name and address of the debtor and the amount owed. Everything else is standardized. The letter should include language to the effect that if the customer does not pay within a certain time frame, other methods of collection will be pursued with their attendant costs and credit implications.

229. Collection agencies are used when appropriate.

Sometimes it is just not worth the effort to pursue a deadbeat customer. When the cost and the hassle are more than the potential recovery, use a collection agency. A collection agency should be used when no one in the company has the personality or expertise to pursue deadbeats. Collection agencies will attempt collection on these accounts for a percentage of the amount collected. After all, half of something is better than all of nothing.

230. All leasing arrangements are reviewed by legal counsel.

Leasing has become a popular way of financing an asset purchase. It is important to understand that leases are legal documents that carry legal responsibilities that are very similar to those accompanying the financing of a purchase at the bank. For this reason, any lease entered into by the company should be reviewed by legal counsel. It can be a very unpleasant revelation when you return your leased vehicle and find out that you owe the leasing company a huge sum of money for excess miles on the vehicle because you were not aware of that provision in the lease.

231. Leases are evaluated for cost-effectiveness.

Leases are generally just purchase contracts with an internal interest rate that the customer does not see. It is important to determine the actual interest rate of the lease contract and compare it to other sources of financing. All terms and conditions of the lease have to be evaluated in order to determine whether leasing is the best alternative for acquiring an asset.

232. Excess funds are in short-term, interest-bearing investments.

The company should not allow large amounts of cash to sit idly in a non-interest-bearing checking account. The company's banker or stockbroker should be able to give the company several good alternatives for the money. It is important to make sure that funds are invested for time periods that will allow the funds to be used when they are needed. This is another good reason to monitor cash flow.

233. Investments are made only with licensed, reputable brokers.

Your son comes to you and tells you that his girlfriend's Aunt Jessica has just found a great investment with a start-up company founded by her neighbor's mother, Teresa. He wants to invest the company's pension plan money or at least the company's excess funds because this deal "could make millions." It sounds ridiculous but millions have been invested in just such a way. There is no reason to invest with anyone other than a licensed and reputable broker, especially if you are the administrator of the company's retirement plan. The alternative could destroy the company and possibly land you in jail.

234. Maturities, yields, and principal balances of investments are carefully monitored.

All aspects of investments need to be monitored by someone who understands the investments. Using a licensed broker will help, but the company controller should know all the important details of any investments made.

235. Employees are cross trained to perform multiple jobs.

Cross training can protect the company when employees leave, take vacations, or become ill. Business cannot just stop because Sue takes maternity leave. At least two people should be proficient in every job function.

236. Workers are employees unless they can substantiate independent contractor status.

Many businesses have tried to avoid workers' compensation insurance and payroll taxes by classifying their employees as independent contractors. This poor management decision can be very costly to a business in penalties, interest, and potential legal liability. All workers are employees unless they can substantiate that they are independent contractors. The IRS has guidelines on this issue if there are any questions. If someone can substantiate that they are an independent contractor, then a simple contract should be signed by both parties as evidence of this relationship.

237. Computer programmer references are checked before the programmer is given access to computer programs.

Just as you would check the references of a potential employee, you should check the references of anyone who is allowed access to your computer system. The damage that could be done to your computer system by an unqualified computer programmer or repair person is frightening.

238. Routine equipment maintenance is performed routinely.

Roger once let his car run out of oil and destroyed the engine block. He now knows why routine equipment maintenance is important. This simple, yet critically important, issue of routine equipment maintenance can save the company thousands of dollars or, alternatively, make the company unable to meet production commitments. In order to ensure that equipment is maintained, the person in charge of maintenance must create a maintenance schedule that is consistently followed.

239. The company complies with all legal notification requirements.

There are laws that dictate the information that must be communicated to employees, customers, and the general public. This information includes payroll and workers' compensation policies, hazardous materials warnings, product ingredients, and so on. The only way to protect your company from legal liability is to follow the law. Ignorance is not an acceptable excuse. Research what is required and comply, rather than find out what you didn't do through a subpoena. Your local chamber of commerce is the best place to start looking for this information.

Insure your assets. Pay for competent advise. Pay attention. Document. Be safe. Use these Power Tools.

Protection

Item	Score	Weight	Power Tool
184		3	Liability insurance is adequate to protect equity.
185		3	Insurance is adequate to prevent personal liability.
186		2	Management is aware of insurance coverage.
187		2	Coverage has been removed from retired assets.
188		2	Limits of coverage are reviewed annually.
189		2	Competitive bids are obtained on insurance.
190		1	Health insurance coverage is competitive.
191		1	Key person life insurance coverage is in place.
192		1	Deductible limits are at the most cost-effective levels.
193		2	Workers' compensation claims are monitored.
194		2	Claims are processed quickly.
195		2	Injured workers are encouraged to return to work ASAP.
196		1	Minor accidents are settled with a liability release.
197		2	Inventories are physically protected from damage or theft.
198		3	Security over fixed assets is adequate.
199		3	Legal counsel is competent and independent.

Item	Score	Weight	Power Tool
200		3	Legal counsel is consulted on all legal issues.
201		3	A competent tax preparer prepares the tax return.
202		3	Correspondence from governmental agencies is handled immediately.
203		3	All tax payments are made on time.
204		2	The company fosters a positive working relationship with its bank.
205		2	The bank is kept informed of the company's operations.
206		3	The company complies with all terms of its loan agreements.
207		2	Banking, legal, and CPA relationships are changed only after careful consideration.
208		3	Management seeks and heeds professional advice in all technical disciplines.
209		2	New employee references are checked.
210		3	Dishonesty of any kind is not tolerated.
211		2	An effective safety program is followed.
212		2	The company complies with all governmental safety policies.
213		3	Hazardous working conditions are not tolerated.
214		2	Computer file backup is performed daily.
215		1	Computer backup is stored off-site.
216		1	An alternate source for data processing is available.
217		2	Data files are password protected.

Item	Score	Weight	Power Tool
218		2	Computer programs are documented, copied, and stored off-site.
219		3	Personnel policies are written.
220		3	Personnel policies are consistently administered.
221		3	One person coordinates personnel policy administration.
222		3	Policies address progressive discipline, discrimination, and harassment.
223		2	All personnel complaints are investigated quickly and completely.
224		2	Everyone's work is subject to review and approval.
225		3	All credit is preapproved and routinely reviewed.
226		2	Past due accounts are monitored weekly.
227		3	Collection procedures are consistent, insistent, and persistent.
228		2	Legal counsel is used to send dunning letters.
229		1	Collection agencies are used when appropriate.
230		3	All leasing arrangements are reviewed by legal counsel.
231		2	Leases are evaluated for cost-effectiveness.
232		1	Excess funds are in short-term, interest-bearing investments.
233		2	Investments are made only with licensed, reputable brokers.
234		2	Maturities, yields, and principal balances of investments are carefully monitored.

Item	Score	Weight	Power Tool
235		2	Employees are cross trained to perform multiple jobs.
236		2	Workers are employees unless they can substantiate independent contractor status.
237		2	Computer programmer references are checked before the programmer is given access to computer programs.
238		1	Routine equipment maintenance is performed routinely.
239		2	The company complies with all legal notification requirements.

6

Production:
Making More with Less

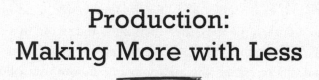

Russ worked for a Fortune 100 aerospace company that man-
ufactures satellites. On rare occasions, he was privileged to see some
of the finished products. It was mind-boggling to ponder what a few
scientists and businesspeople had accomplished. They had accumulated some of the brightest engineering minds in the country. They
produced cutting-edge technology which provided instantaneous
communication to the most remote corners of the world, but it took
the company seven days to receive a filing cabinet and deliver it
across the street. Russ was assigned to remedy that problem.

During his evaluation, he determined that the problem wasn't in
Receiving, but in the way one department dealt with another. This
is common in many large businesses. As an organization grows, it
departmentalizes into controllable units. Each department then creates separate objectives and policies to facilitate management. Re-
grettably, in many cases, these distinctions form barriers to the other
departments. Infighting ensues and the departments forget the ultimate objective. Design, purchasing, receiving, accounting, and production are important, but none is an end in and of itself.

By using the Power Tools presented in this chapter, Russ was able to speed up the receiving process and contribute to the profitability of the company as a whole. Yours might not be a huge company, but you should be able to apply most of these Power Tools.

240. The employees understand the company's organization.

According to a popular comedian, "If your family tree doesn't fork . . . , you may be a 'Red Neck.' " In many family businesses the organizational chart looks just like the family tree. Dad and Mom are at the top, then the kids, then their kids, and so on. In a company that we consulted, the owner said that everyone reported to him: the shop hand, the secretary, the job foreman, and the controller. It was no wonder his desk was a mess, orders were always late, and he was very grumpy. There needs to be a logical, efficient, organization.

It's a good idea to create an organizational chart. Seeing in print where one fits into the organization promotes a sense of belonging. Define things that need to be done and assign the most qualified people to be responsible for those tasks. This should reduce misunderstanding among family members and show all employees where they fit in the organization and to whom they report. Make sure you distribute the organizational chart to every employee.

241. Employees are taught how their tasks help the company to achieve its objectives.

Dad had an employee named Jimmy who took great pride in stocking his assigned aisles. The cans and boxes of dog food stood in perfectly straight rows like orchards of fruit trees or fields of corn. Jimmy taught Russ to pull the cans from the back so the shelves always looked full. "No one likes to buy from an empty cart," he would say. Russ came to resent the customers who would buy the product and disturb the pristine displays. That demonstrates a flaw in his education process. The purpose of making a display, or packaging a product, or sweeping the floor is to entice a customer to buy.

How often have you gone into a store where a frantic clerk crouches among a pile of cartons and completely ignores you while labeling and stacking merchandise? When employees are taught what the objectives of the company are and how the employees help achieve those objectives, then customer service improves. If it is difficult for you to determine how someone's job helps the company achieve its objectives, then you should probably eliminate that job.

242. Employees benefit from the company achieving its objectives.

Why do private-sector employees traditionally outperform public employees? Many public employees perceive that their jobs are protected, they have no quotas, their services are expected not appreciated, and there is no incentive to do any better. In your family business, you have the power to motivate your employees by giving them incentives to accomplish your objectives.

We know of a plumbing company that had a terrible safety record. Workers' compensation rates were going through the roof. Even worse, they were losing productive employees to illness and injury. The owners' objective was to reduce injuries by 90 percent. They started a drawing of $50 for the workers with no reported injuries in a month's period. Because fifty bucks was not sufficient incentive to some employees, once a year they had a drawing for a trip to Hawaii. Only one prize was awarded at a time, but everyone worked for the chance to win. It cost the company less than $3,000 for an insurance savings of over $60,000. Different incentives work for different people: cash, days off, recognition, praise, company T-shirts . . . . Try the ones that don't cost any money first.

243. Authority is delegated with responsibility.

Remember Deputy Barney Fife on *The Andy Griffith Show*? For obvious reasons, he was only allowed one bullet for his gun. Barney got very little respect because people knew he couldn't back up his threats. Do you have responsible people with no bullets? Can your supervisors initiate disciplinary action with employees? Does manufacturing have sufficient purchasing authority to meet quotas? Can your salespeople give discounts for quantity purchases? Authority is a tool like a hammer or a calculator. You shouldn't ask employees to do a job if you don't trust them with the necessary tools.

Productivity is achieved through proper delegation. There are hundreds of reasons why owners are reluctant to delegate authority. The basic reason is fear: fear of losing control, fear of being obsolete, fear that the employee won't perform. By giving assignments that require the owner's approval at each step, the owner ties him or herself into the process. That's like shackling a racehorse to the starting gate. A better means of mitigating the owner's fear is to place limits on authority. Budgets are used to control spending, quantities are established for sales cost reductions, and dollar limits are set for check approvals and purchasing limits.

244. All ideas for improvement are entertained.

A high school in Arizona was plagued by a teenage fad. The girls determined that it was cute to make lipstick kisses on the mirrors. The problem became epidemic, and the teachers became really concerned when the lipstick started showing up in the boys' bathrooms. The teachers and aides started watches, the administration performed studies, the keenest educators in the county were consulted on how to end this messy obsession. All the while, a humble janitor affirmed that she had the solution. The educators finally gave in and allowed the janitor to try her scheme.

One day while a group of girls was loitering in the rest room, the janitor entered and excused herself as she began to clean. She dipped her mop into the toilet and scrubbed the lipstick off the mirror. The girls squealed "Omagosh" and thus the scarlet smooches ended.

There is always room for improvement. Your people know best

what's wrong with your business. Don't dismiss a suggestion because of its origin.

245. Everyone is treated with dignity.

In college, Russ attended the lecture of a prominent sociologist who studied world religions. He pointed out the great diversity among sects, but also that there was a prevailing concept among the majority of faiths: Do unto others as you would have others do to you. This is evidence of an almost universal belief of humankind. J. C. Penney started his family's retail business using the name "The Golden Rule Store." It doesn't matter what name is on the door, if people are treated with dignity and respect, they will most often respond in kind.

246. Employees are given feedback on all ideas.

Your evaluation of an idea is just one step in the improvement process. Whether or not you incorporate the idea, the presenter should receive feedback. This acknowledges the individual's contribution. The process of explaining your reasoning to the employee will also solidify your relationship with the employee.

247. Employees receive verbal and monetary rewards for input.

Hughes Aircraft has a reward system for employee input. Employees receive points for every idea the company uses, based on the benefit to the business. The points are presented by the employee's supervisor as a certificate to be redeemed for consumer merchandise through an outside company that administers the incentive program. Each point is only worth a few cents, but the ideas presented have saved the company literally millions of dollars. The idea originator receives both verbal and monetary rewards for helping the company.

You may choose a profit-sharing plan as a way of rewarding your employees. Even then, verbal expression of appreciation is just as important.

248. Performance evaluations are held regularly.

Large companies tend to have very formal human resource procedures. That's probably because they have people with the time to administer these procedures. One of the best things that has come from their observations and brainstorming is the performance evaluation. These interviews can be the most productive interactions with your employees. The interviews are definitely worth the investment of your time. An average full-time employee spends 1,985 hours a year at work. An annual performance evaluation costs, at most, an hour. If that hour could increase productivity just 3 percent, think of the return to the company.

The interviews should be face-to-face, allow both people to express their concerns, and end on a positive note. You should be specific as to where, when, and to what degree you expect improvement. The evaluations must be scheduled at least once a year so they are not overlooked.

249. Poor performance is constructively criticized.

Whether you're related or not, your employees should be extensions of you. They should expand your ability to get the job done. They should help you be more successful. Once in a while, employees will fall short of your expectations. When they do, there is a right way and a wrong way of letting them know. The right way does not include the terms "numskull," "dimwit," "dingbat," or "airhead."

Recognize the difference between an occurrence and a continuing problem, then treat the person accordingly. When dealing with a poor performer, it is best to concentrate on the task and not the individual. Try "Our customers need someone here to answer their calls at eight o'clock. Are you that person?" rather than "Be here by eight or you're fired." The desired behavior and consequence are communicated in both statements, but the first gives employees control and is less likely to create an enemy in the ranks.

250. Consistently poor performance is penalized.

Some old-school managers might think modern personnel policies are namby-pamby psycho-nonsense. We live in a litigious and sometimes violent society. Keeping a cool head is the best policy. But that's not to say that you shouldn't reprimand an employee who consistently performs poorly. On the contrary, it is your duty. Every business should have and follow a policy of progressive discipline. This policy should include warnings, days off without pay, and ultimately termination. Two more things to consider: be consistent and keep records.

251. Quality performance is rewarded.

A good manager tries to make bad employees good and good employees better. A pat on the back, a parking place, or a paid day off are small incremental investments in greater productivity. These can be leveraged by spotlighting outstanding employees in front of their peers. Let everyone know whom you consider to be a good employee and show the others the rewards. Be careful to quantify the desired behaviors; for example, "Mary is getting this day off because she has produced more widgets than any other employee." The other employees may know that Mary is always late for work and begrudge her reward, but they can't argue with her quantified performance.

252. People are considered the company's most valuable resource.

In our transitional economy, not many businesses can boast a huge war chest of money. Large inventories tie up capital. Technology makes state-of-the-art equipment obsolete almost overnight. A bank can call a loan due and investors are easily lured away. Inventories, equipment, loans and people are resources with associated problems, but people should be considered your most valuable resource. They are the source of innovation, they get the work done, they make you money.

One element common in many bankrupt companies where we have consulted is that the people are devalued by the actions of the owner; sometimes even the owner's children are devalued. We have seen capable people whose ideas were not considered. They were lorded over and told they were too stupid to help. We have also seen troubled companies where the people worked without pay and sacrificed to help the owner. The difference was how they were treated. Often, the money isn't as important as friendship and loyalty. People are your most valuable resource. Treat them that way.

253. Personnel problems are resolved as they arise.

Don't sweep problems under the rug. It is easier to clean up a little mess when it's found, than a big mess that has accumulated over time. Your company's productivity is a function of your employees' productivity. Unhappy employees are not productive. Lack of action can also lead to some very messy lawsuits filed by employees.

254. Employees are trained in problem resolution.

A package arrived at the receiving dock. The receiving clerk examined the package and attempted to match the packing list with an invoice on the computer. There was no matching purchase order so the clerk set the package aside. The buyer had made a verbal order to the vendor, but had not input the order into the computer system. The vendor had responded quickly, shipped the order, and mailed the invoice the same day. A month later the vendor called Accounting to request payment. Accounting replied that there was no record of receipt and referred the vendor to the buyer. Meanwhile the box sat on the receiving dock gathering dust and the requester was irritated at the vendor for not shipping the order.

No matter how sophisticated your systems, there will be problems. In this case, at least four people's time was wasted looking for a box that was sitting on the receiving dock. If someone had taught the receiving clerk that the purchase order number on the packing list designates who the buyer is, this problem could have been resolved with a single phone call.

Teach your people the system and be careful that they don't bypass it. With good people and good systems in place, your time will not be spent resolving problems.

255. Performance expectations are communicated to the employees.

During a performance evaluation Russ indicated that he was not happy with the way a salesperson had treated a customer. In her defense, the saleswoman pointed out that unlike some of the other salespeople, she was always there on time, often stayed late, and hadn't taken any of her vacation. She was almost shocked at the reply. Russ told her that he appreciated that she came to work on time and her extra efforts, but he expected her to take her time off, and serving the customers was much more important than punching a time clock.

Sometimes producing to expectations is more important than whether the employee comes to work on time. You know what you want from your employees, so tell them. Build on their good habits, though. When Russ evaluated the other salespeople, he praised their productivity and discussed their tardiness.

256. All employees participate in ongoing training programs.

When she was hired, the lady who works at our front desk was not proficient on our computer software. At first she would bring her questions to us and, we admit, we had to study to find the answers. It was a learning process for all of us. We purchased a *Word Perfect for Dummies* manual and then subscribed to a monthly tutorial magazine. Now she works independently and answers our questions. Ongoing training does not have to be fancy or expensive, but it is usually productive. You don't have to know how to do everything, just how to get your employees trained.

257. Productivity gains do not cause termination of good workers.

"Doctor, it hurts when I do this." "Then don't do that." If your employees see their peers get fired when production increases, how long do you think they will work at peak capacity? The objective of improving productivity is not to reduce labor expense; it is to reduce the percent of labor cost to sales revenue. Channel the energies of a good worker into another area. Good people are hard to find; don't let them get away because you're producing more with fewer employees.

258. All managers are responsible for productivity.

President Harry S. Truman had a sign on his desk, "The Buck Stops Here." Managers shouldn't pass the buck. A manager should have specific areas of responsibility and be held accountable for the productivity of that area.

"Manager" is not an honorary title. It should indicate that the person has and continues to demonstrate a high level of responsibility. When Russ was assigned to clean up a receiving and inspection department, he displaced a manager who was twenty-five years his senior. The manager had remained inconspicuous for some time. Early on-the-job retirement can be a bigger problem in a family business, where it hurts to put beloved relatives out to pasture. While love and respect should be prevailing values in a family-owned business, the long-term vision of the company must be paramount. If you let your concern for one person override what is best for everyone in the company, the company will fail.

When tackling the challenge of utilizing an aging relative, consider the following things. The threat of young pups nipping at heels might motivate more productivity, or these relatives could serve effectively as board members or project consultants. When people age, they often like to return to what they did best in the past. Uncle Lyman, the former CFO, might be both happy and productive working with accounts receivable.

259. The company is neat, clean, and orderly.

Here's a tip from two business consultants that most consultants don't want you to know: you can save thousands of dollars on consulting fees simply by becoming more organized. Clean up your shop or yard. Sell old vehicles and scrap old equipment. Recycle paper and other supplies. Don't leave cash lying around; establish a petty cash account. Label your files. File pending orders and information. Follow IRS guidelines and purge outdated records. Buy some shelving and get those boxes off the ground. Reduce sticky note reminders and use a calendar. Don't save junk parts thinking that you will repair them; sell or trash them.

In a turnaround situation, the first things we do are physical. A coat of paint, some soap and elbow grease can do wonders for morale. Clearing driveways and access ways increases mobility. A new professionally painted sign draws new business. Sometimes rearranging the desks can give employees and management a new perspective. Don't forget to look behind the cushions for change; every little bit helps.

260. Redundancies are eliminated by handling a transaction the fewest times possible.

Brady, Melody, and Katy worked for a warehouse equipment wholesale business. Brady worked in the warehouse, but he would often help out on the order desk. He didn't type, so when he took orders he would write them on an order pad. Because his handwriting was illegible, he would often print the order on a new form and put it in a basket to be typed. Katy did the typing, but she was not familiar with the catalog so she would often ask Melody for clarification. Melody did the books and was experienced in all the office procedures. Thus orders would often be handled by three different people before leaving the office. Katy would sometimes type both the draft and final rewrite of Brady's orders, causing the warehouse to duplicate the order. Melody was good, but with constant interruptions she occasionally made input errors.

Every time someone lays down an unfinished transaction, someone else has to pick it up and reread that same item. There are many solutions to this scenario, including training, reassignment of duties, using part numbers, better organization of the catalog, purchasing a computer for direct order input, and separating bookkeeping from the order desk. Every area of a business should be evaluated for efficiency.

261. Employees are provided with the tools they need to do the job.

We know a manager who was so stingy with a buck that he wouldn't buy a new broom for his shop. We came on the scene and witnessed a union shop hand pushing iron shavings with a broom that looked like a thirteen-year-old's mustache. Union shop hands can make $25 per hour plus benefits. The owner could have purchased several brooms with the wages wasted using inferior equipment. The right tools make people more productive.

Some managers require their employees to provide their own tools. In many cases, personal responsibility is enhanced when the employee feels a financial stake in the activity. A more even-handed approach may be to provide the first set of tools and require the employee to make any replacements.

262. Management style fosters creativity by encouraging employees to ask "Is there a better way?"

This tool is designed to require some introspection. It is a constant endeavor to motivate others, but we should have control of ourselves. Start with your own style, the way you interrelate with your employees. Are you approachable? Do you really listen to your subordinates? Do you act on improvement recommendations? Are you abrupt or distracted when someone approaches you? Are you overly protective of your systems or processes? Are you condescending to your subordinates? Do you use statements like "Don't ever question me" or "Don't think, just do what you're told"?

If you want the best out of your employees, the person to start with may be the one who looks back at you in the mirror.

263. The company rejects perfection in favor of action.

We were all raised with the adage "A job worth doing is worth doing well." When Russ was starting his career, he had a boss who taught him a different perspective. He would say, "A job worth doing is worth doing *poorly*." In other words, if a job needs to be done, *it should be done* even if it can't be perfect. This man was not one to accept mediocrity. He was a teaching administrator at a large hospital and internationally known for his work in human fertility.

Russ understood his perspective immediately. Russ was in college with a heavy course load, married with a child on the way, and trying to support his little family with night jobs and contract work. With more responsibilities than time, he knew something had to give. At times he settled for C's when he might have had A's in college. If he had given up his education because he wasn't an A student, he would not have developed the rich, rewarding life he enjoys today. Business is no different. When juggling the many responsibilities, you must recognize that things have to get done even if they're not done perfectly.

Our friend runs a mail presorting business. The sorting equipment sits on tables that he made himself out of plywood. He designed the tables with jigs and grooves to assist the input operators. These tables aren't beautiful. Perfect tables would have been laminated or painted, but our friend chose function over appearance and got the job done. If he had chosen to wait for perfect equipment, the business might now be out of business.

264. A logical flow of activities is defined and communicated to employees.

They called it the "Black Hole of Production." Parts were delivered there and never came out. To shed some light on the problem, Russ created a flowchart to chronicle each step in the production, inspection, and transportation process. He highlighted the rules that the other departments most often broke. When the chart was finished, he had each department manager verify its accuracy. Then he evaluated the flowchart looking for redundancies or loops and obsolete requirements.

The visual presentation made it easy for all involved to see where the process breakdowns occurred. By working together on the entire process and not just the individual departments, they were able to improve productivity up to 90 percent. We strongly recommend that each identifiable process be flowcharted and evaluated. This will also help teach new employees more quickly how things are done.

265. Activities are standardized.

We buy brand names, stay in chain hotels, and eat at franchise restaurants because we know that what we order will be the same quality as when we ordered it before. Russ went into a Kentucky Fried Chicken outlet in Sao Paulo, Brazil. The chicken, potatoes, and coleslaw tasted exactly the same as in our hometown of Torrance, California. The secret is not the chicken recipe, but the standardization of the business practices.

It is unlikely that you will ever become rich by owning a small retail shop. The shop may provide your immediate family with a nice living, but there may not be enough business to support the families of your grown children. If you create processes that produce quality results and can be reproduced again and again, you could provide your children with a business of their own in an area where they choose to live. This should extend into every aspect of your business. Then, just as on Henry Ford's assembly line, every job is interchangeable, with minimal training or effort required.

266. The transfer of responsibility is standardized and understood by all parties.

Is there an In box on your secretary's desk? Does everybody use the In box or do they lay things on the desk blotter or, if they're really important, on the chair? In some businesses, the employees think that dropping paperwork in the Out box in front of them means that they have no more responsibility for it. These handoffs are like a relay race. The teams that standardize their handoffs normally come out the winners.

Don't let your employees pass the buck by saying, "I gave that to Mary to do" when Mary has never seen it. Make sure all employees know what is required to complete their assignments and how to notify the next person that responsibility has been transferred. Standardizing handoffs also frees the supervisor from constantly giving orders or passing out assignments.

267. Immediate action is taken to correct product flaws.

An amazing phenomenon occurs every February in Quartzsite, Arizona. The population grows by hundreds of thousands of snowbirds in RVs. They go there to ride out the winter and enjoy the Gem and Mineral Show, a big trade show for the lapidary industry. The retired couples love to find bargains, so many tool manufacturers go there to sell their substandard products. Russ was the marketing manager for one such manufacturer. People would complain that the company didn't have the selection that they used to have. That was because the company's new owner understood the importance of correcting product flaws.

The company's previous owner concentrated on high-volume production but did not monitor the processes. He had hundreds of rejects. He was losing thousands of dollars because he had to sell his rejects at a substantial discount. The new owner quickly corrected product flaws, reduced the number of rejects, and increased his profit margin.

It takes much less money to do the job right than to do it twice. If you don't immediately correct product flaws, you have but three legitimate choices: remake the defective product, sell it at a discount, or scrap it. You lose money any way you look at it.

268. Records are kept of product returns and quality problems.

Our church runs a volunteer cannery to provide food to needy families. One of our assignments there was to keep track of the lid numbers used in each batch of cans produced. Should a flaw be detected, management could trace the product by the lid number to the day, shift, and batch of origin. This simple accounting could save a business thousands of dollars. In the event of a flaw, only a bad batch will be recalled, instead of all the products produced. A record of returns should also be kept to identify recurring problems.

269. Products are engineered for ease in manufacture.

There are many things we can learn from good manufacturing practices. In larger companies, Marketing identifies a needed product, Design creates a working model, and then the manufacturing engineers redesign the product so it can be economically reproduced. They ask questions like "How can we produce this with the fewest pieces possible?" "Where can we reduce materials and still provide a product the market can support?" "How much of the process can we mechanize to reduce labor cost?" "How can we help the workforce manipulate the product for ease in production?"

All industries can reengineer their products using these principles: make it simple; make it economical; mechanize.

270. Monotonous tasks are periodically reassigned or distributed to several employees.

ZZZZZZZZZZZZZZZZZ. There are very few things less productive than a worker who is bored. Your people may literally be running, with sweat dripping from their brows, but if they are tired of their jobs or feel they are monotonous, then they are not giving you 100 percent. They are thinking about their weekend, planning a party, or watching the clock. With their minds somewhere else, they are more likely to cause an accident, get injured, not show up for work, or make mistakes. When this happens, it's not just low productivity but counterproductivity.

To avoid boredom in the workplace, it's a good idea to shake things up once in a while. Pass around the mailers to be stuffed, cross-train your manufacturing workers, let someone else pick up the mail. Some people may consider assignment to a monotonous task to be a punishment, but if they see that everyone is pitching in, it will be considered more of a break.

271.   Work areas are ergonomically designed.

If ergonomic was a word when we were in college, it was never discussed. Russ first saw it in an advertisement for office furniture. To be ergonomic means to be comfortable and convenient to a person. Russ often worked at a client's office where the phone was positioned on the credenza behind the desk. Russ would often wrap himself up in the cord or drag the phone until it went crashing to the ground. It wasn't convenient to the way he worked.

We've also seen a direct mail company that kept literature across the room because that's where the shelving fit. Every time a request came in, the clerk would get up and walk across the room to fill the order.

Put the tools and materials close to the work stations of the people who use them most. Buy or make shelves, clamps, or brackets that bring things to comfortable working levels. These aids may cost money, but they are an investment in productivity.

272.   Management and employees understand it is cheaper to do the job right the first time.

The production team was one batch away from achieving the highest quota ever produced in a month. There were sufficient parts to achieve the goal but the plating process wouldn't allow time to clean the parts. The supervisor made the decision to rely on the supplier's cleaning process and push the product through. Everyone was so happy with their bonus for achieving such a high objective. The boss patted himself on the back, thinking, I knew they could reach that quota.

Now let's count the costs. Five dozen parts were shipped before Customer Service alerted Shipping of a defect. Thirty customers were lost because they received inferior parts. Who knows how many people they told about their bad experience? Quality Assurance had to reinspect all the batches made for two weeks around that batch date. Manufacturing had to work overtime to strip the bad batch and clean the parts correctly. The list goes on and on.

Management must establish objectives, but it is always cheaper to do the job right the first time.

273. Customers are given realistic delivery dates.

Everyone wants to please the customer. Sometimes, to make a sale, a delivery date is promised which pushes Production beyond its capabilities. When the delivery date passes and the product has not been delivered, the customer is mad. That is just where the pebble hits the water; let's consider the ripple effect. An unrealistic delivery date stresses the workforce, potentially causing accidents, promoting shortcuts which can create defects, derailing other promised delivery dates, and ultimately demoralizing workers.

274. Delays are communicated to customers.

Customers want their product delivered on time. If you cannot deliver as promised, you must inform the customer. There are some delays over which you have no control. We have waited weeks for custom orders without so much as a phone call from the supplier. We appreciate a vendor who calls to say their parts supplier can't deliver until next Thursday. It's even better when they call the next Thursday to say they have received the parts and will call again on Monday with a firm delivery date.

Customers will put up with a lot if you are honest with them. You owe it to your customers to tell them when you can't deliver so they can make other arrangements.

This is a good customer relations practice, but it can also encourage greater productivity. Accountability is a strong motivator. If your Production Department knows that every day they go over the specified delivery date they have to call the customer and explain why, they will be more motivated to get the job done.

275. Production scheduling allows management to determine the status of each job in progress.

There are a lot of good cooks in our town but there are only a few good caterers. The difference is not in the recipes but in the caterer's ability to manage multiple jobs. One client of ours has developed a system and he always sticks to it. He works backward from the delivery date and defines each step in the process of filling each order. He identifies similar activities and combines them. If you're set up to mash ten dozen potatoes, why not mash fifty dozen? His kitchen is organized into workstations and he doesn't overschedule them. Sometimes he has to work overtime to complete a job, but his schedule allows him to build that into the price and pass it on to the client. The crew is informed about their next assignment in advance with a posted order sheet. They don't waste time waiting for instructions. When one process is done, they immediately set up the next.

Good scheduling allows you to establish better pricing, control overtime expense, reduce labor costs, and eliminate unproductive time.

Remember that people are the key to production. Organize. Reward good performance. Do it right the first time. Communicate. The following Production Power Tools chart will complete the evaluation of your business.

Production

Item	Score	Weight	Power Tool
240		2	The employees understand the company's organization.
241		2	Employees are taught how their tasks help the company to achieve its objectives.
242		3	Employees benefit from the company achieving its objectives.
243		3	Authority is delegated with responsibility.
244		2	All ideas for improvement are entertained.
245		3	Everyone is treated with dignity.
246		2	Employees are given feedback on all ideas.
247		2	Employees receive verbal and monetary rewards for input.
248		3	Performance evaluations are held regularly.
249		3	Poor performance is constructively criticized.
250		2	Consistently poor performance is penalized.
251		3	Quality performance is rewarded.
252		3	People are considered the company's most valuable resource.
253		2	Personnel problems are resolved as they arise.
254		2	Employees are trained in problem resolution.
255		2	Performance expectations are communicated to the employees.

Item	Score	Weight	Power Tool
256		2	All employees participate in ongoing training programs.
257		2	Productivity gains do not cause termination of good workers.
258		3	All managers are responsible for productivity.
259		2	The company is neat, clean, and orderly.
260		3	Redundancies are eliminated by handling a transaction the fewest times possible.
261		2	Employees are provided with the tools they need to do the job.
262		2	Management style fosters creativity by encouraging employees to ask ''Is there a better way?''
263		2	The company rejects perfection in favor of action.
264		3	A logical flow of activities is defined and communicated to employees.
265		2	Activities are standardized.
266		3	The transfer of responsibility is standardized and understood by all parties.
267		3	Immediate action is taken to correct product flaws.
268		2	Records are kept of product returns and quality problems.
269		2	Products are engineered for ease in manufacture.
270		2	Monotonous tasks are periodically reassigned or distributed to several employees.
271		1	Work areas are ergonomically designed.

Item	Score	Weight	Power Tool
272		3	Management and employees understand it is cheaper to do the job right the first time.
273		2	Customers are given realistic delivery dates.
274		2	Delays are communicated to customers.
275		3	Production scheduling allows management to determine the status of each job in progress.

7
Creating the Plan of Attack

A couple years ago we saw a movie about three yuppies who sought an adventure on a cattle drive. In the midst of their comical trials, the sage and imposing trail boss taught a philosophical lesson. He raised his callused index finger and said, "One thing—that's all you have to think about." In our complex business environment, that is a luxury none of us can afford, but there is merit in reducing our concerns to a manageable few.

We have explained 275 Power Tools. You are undoubtedly using most of them in your business. In the Introduction of this book under the "How to Use This Book" heading, we explained the Power Tools system for scoring your performance. The following will help you implement your Power Tools system:

1. You should have scored your business in each of the 275 Power Tools listed at the end of each chapter. If not, use the Appendix and do that now.
2. Highlight each Power Tool with a Score of 0 and a Weight of 3.
3. Work on these Power Tools until you can give yourself a score of 2.

4. Repeat the process for the Power Tools with a Score of 0 and a Weight of 2.

5. Continue the process until you can give yourself a 2 for all of the Power Tools.

We recommend that the owner complete the Power Tools system first. Then each of the business' key personnel should do the same. These perspectives may differ and may give everyone new insight into the needs of the business.

Our experience has been that you will have four or five Power Tools in each category that you need to work on. Use your judgment to prioritize them.

A Blueprint for Survival, Success, and Succession

You are the architect of your future. You have been given 275 Power Tools that will make building your business easier. This book should have helped you create a blueprint for a successful family business. Now go and create a legacy.

Power Tools Software

We have developed a software program to help you implement the Power Tools system. You simply input your scores and the software organizes the Power Tools in the order you should follow. It also gives you a percentage score to compare how you are doing in each category: Family, Marketing, Management, Accounting, Protection, and Production.

**To order Power Tools Action Plan Software
call (888) 4-ALLRED.
(425-5733)**

We have helped many family businesses. Your success is important to us. If we can be of assistance to you, please call us at the same number. We would be pleased to present our Power Tools Seminar to your trade organization or chamber of commerce.

Appendix
Power Tools, Listed in Order

Family

Item	Score	Weight	Power Tool
1		3	The family business has the four essential plans for survival, success and succession.
2		3	The family has a mission statement for the business.
3		3	The family has a vision statement for the business.
4		2	Family values and objectives are incorporated into the strategic plan of the business.
5		2	Management knows the objectives of the family.
6		2	Family business meetings are held regularly.
7		3	Family members are competent in their assignments.

Item	Score	Weight	Power Tool
8		2	Family members are compensated according to their contribution to the business.
9		2	Performance standards are the same for family and non-family employees.
10		2	Family disputes are handled in a predetermined manner so as not to inhibit operations.
11		1	Children who will work in the family business start working in the business at a young age.
12		1	The family requires children who will work in the business to have an education that will benefit the business.
13		1	Children who will work in the family business are required to work for another business for a period of time.
14		1	Mentors are used to develop family members' abilities.
15		3	Non-family managers are used in the absence of qualified family members.
16		3	The business is protected from the effects of divorce or death of the owners.
17		1	The family has a plan to deal with the death or disability of family employees.
18		3	The family has identified the successor to the current president.
19		2	There is a time scheduled for the president to retire.
20		3	There is a plan to transfer the business to the next generation.
21		2	There is a method to determine which members of the family can work for, own stock in, or be on the Board of Directors of the business.

Item	Score	Weight	Power Tool
22		2	The company has buy/sell agreements.
23		1	There is control on the number and value of luxury items purchased by the business for employees.
24		1	The family has a network of other family business owners with which they share experiences and exchange information.
25		2	Discipline is the same for family and non-family members.
26		2	Responsibility and authority of non-family managers is not undermined.

Marketing

Item	Score	Weight	Power Tool
27		3	All understand that sales is their major function.
28		1	Management knows the customers.
29		3	Management has personal contact with large customers on a regular basis.
30		2	Management is dedicated to quality service and products.
31		1	All employees have access to appropriate promotional materials for distribution.
32		3	The company has a written marketing plan.
33		2	The marketing plan includes quantifiable markets.
34		2	The marketing plan is reviewed regularly.

Item	Score	Weight	Power Tool
35		2	The marketing plan identifies the target markets.
36		2	The marketing plan includes a detailed budget.
37		3	Advertising is focused on the target market.
38		2	Advertising cost is evaluated by the lowest cost per target market contact.
39		2	Unplanned promotional costs are reviewed by management for focus and return on investment.
40		3	Management has defined an image for the company.
41		2	The image is appealing to its target customers.
42		2	The image is portrayed in all promotional materials.
43		1	The image is reflected in the company premises.
44		1	The image is fostered by all employees.
45		3	Promotional media are appropriate for the product or service.
46		2	Promotional media follow a standard theme.
47		2	Promotional media are informative yet not overly wordy.
48		2	Promotional media make it easy to see what you are selling.
49		1	Promotional media affect as many senses as possible.
50		2	All promotional media and activities are designed to satisfy the needs of the customer.

Item	Score	Weight	Power Tool
51		2	No conflicting logos or insignia are distributed.
52		3	The company is accessible to its customers.
53		2	The telephone system is adequate for the number of calls received.
54		3	The telephone is answered promptly and responsibly.
55		3	Initial contact is courteous and friendly.
56		1	Messages are always returned.
57		2	Signs are legible and obvious.
58		1	Parking is adequate.
59		3	Pricing is as high as the market will bear.
60		2	Demographics are reviewed annually for future market planning.
61		3	Sales objectives are established at least annually and identified by month.
62		2	Sales objectives are realistic.
63		2	Follow up, follow up, follow up.
64		1	Sales are tracked by territory.
65		3	Sales staff is friendly, knowledgeable, helpful, and courteous.
66		2	Sales staff is familiar with the competition's product.
67		3	Sales staff takes the time to listen to the client's needs before trying to sell a product.
68		2	The market for new products is examined monthly.

Item	Score	Weight	Power Tool
69		3	New markets for existing products are considered regularly.
70		2	Market trends are examined monthly.
71		2	Sales trends are analyzed monthly by the sales manager.
72		2	Radical changes in trend are examined in detail.
73		2	All customer complaints are investigated quickly and completely.
74		2	Dissatisfied customers receive a courteous and personal response.
75		1	Selling costs are compared to gross margin on sales.

Management

Item	Score	Weight	Power Tool
76		1	Management directs the business in a positive manner.
77		3	Management is dedicated to long-term profitability.
78		3	Management's integrity is beyond reproach.
79		2	Management is goal oriented.
80		2	The company has a logical organization.
81		2	The company has written standards and objectives.

Item	Score	Weight	Power Tool
82		3	Responsibility is delegated to the lowest level possible.
83		2	Delegated authority is not superseded without absolute need.
84		2	Management support of supervisors is apparent to all.
85		2	The company has regular management meetings.
86		2	The company has regular staff meetings.
87		2	All suggestions are noted and carefully considered.
88		1	Ideas are acted on quickly.
89		2	"Trials" are not held to place blame for mistakes.
90		1	Managers "wander around" to keep in touch with employees.
91		2	Management expects good performance.
92		2	Staffing levels are reviewed regularly.
93		2	There is little excess personnel capacity.
94		2	Overtime is planned and controlled.
95		3	Decreases in staffing levels are handled fairly and with extreme care.
96		1	Excess files, computer programs, procedures, etc. are identified and eliminated.
97		1	The company is not a victim of "paralysis through analysis."
98		1	The company makes a reasonable number of mistakes.
99		2	Customers are billed immediately after delivery.

Item	Score	Weight	Power Tool
100		3	Managers take care of their personal lives.
101		2	Profit margins are sufficient for each product.
102		1	Profit margins are tracked monthly.
103		3	Net margins exceed alternate investment yields.
104		2	Major costs are identified.
105		2	Cost cutting efforts concentrate on major costs.
106		3	Any change is reviewed for cost/benefit relationship.
107		2	Reducing costs is an ongoing effort.
108		2	No area is exempt from cost-cutting review.
109		2	Financial trends are examined monthly.
110		2	Any change in financial trends is examined in detail.
111		2	Large variances in any account are explained.
112		3	Cash flow is analyzed monthly.
113		1	Cash flow is monitored daily.
114		1	Inventory levels are analyzed for trends.
115		1	Obsolete inventory is identified for liquidation.
116		2	Inventory is purchased according to a plan.
117		2	Cash flow will support the inventory plan.
118		2	Carrying/handling costs do not exceed profit margins.

Item	Score	Weight	Power Tool
119		1	Inventory is ordered for just-in-time delivery.
120		2	Purchase orders are issued only by authorized employees.
121		1	Purchasing is independent of operations and accounts payable.
122		2	Goods are approved as they are received.
123		1	The purchase order is matched to the receiving report and invoice.
124		2	Competitive bids are obtained on all large purchases.
125		1	Subcontractors are used whenever cost effective.
126		2	Capital expenditures are prioritized.
127		2	Management negotiates to reduce costs.
128		2	Reasonable forecasts are used as a basis for budgets.
129		3	Budgets are used to monitor sales and expenditures.
130		2	Budgets are used to project cash flow and debt service.
131		1	Purchase discounts are taken if the annualized rate exceeds the borrowing rate.
132		2	Management is committed to a drug-free workplace.
133		2	Management knows that the only thing that is constant is change.

Accounting

Item	Score	Weight	Power Tool
134		3	Monthly financial statements are prepared.
135		3	Monthly financial statements are reviewed by management.
136		2	Monthly financial statements are timely.
137		3	Monthly financial statements are accurate.
138		2	Monthly financial statements reflect company operations.
139		2	Cash accounts are reconciled regularly.
140		1	All accounts are shown on the general ledger.
141		1	Unreconciled items are resolved.
142		2	Check signers are appropriate in number and responsibility.
143		3	All money received is deposited daily.
144		3	Management reviews cash receipts and disbursements.
145		1	Disbursements are consistently approved for payment.
146		3	Disbursements are made only with adequate supporting documentation.
147		3	Checks are signed only after reviewing supporting documents.
148		1	Supporting documents are always cancelled when paid.
149		2	Disbursements are consistently posted to the proper accounts.
150		2	Accounts payable are posted and disbursements are made on time.

Item	Score	Weight	Power Tool
151		2	Accounts receivable subsidiary ledger totals agree with the general ledger.
152		1	Statements of accounts are mailed monthly.
153		2	All customers are on the aged accounts receivable.
154		2	All accounts are aged accurately.
155		2	Profit margins are determinable.
156		2	Periodic physical inventories are consistently taken.
157		2	Book inventories are reconciled to physical inventories.
158		1	Inventory reconciliation is immediately performed.
159		2	The physical inventory agrees with the general ledger.
160		1	Inventories are valued at the lower of cost or market value.
161		2	The capitalization policy is followed.
162		1	The fixed asset ledger is maintained.
163		2	Fixed assets are properly set up and depreciated.
164		1	Fixed assets are properly retired.
165		1	Fixed asset inventories are taken.
166		2	The balance sheet is in balance.
167		2	Income shown on the income statement equals the increase in equity on the balance sheet.
168		3	The income statement reflects only actual income.

Item	Score	Weight	Power Tool
169		2	The income statement is sufficiently detailed.
170		1	Account titles are accurate and specific.
171		2	Prepaid accounts are adjusted to actual amounts.
172		3	The type of business organization is correct.
173		2	Detailed records are maintained on all active accounts.
174		2	Equity and Draw accounts are reconciled monthly.
175		1	Suspense accounts are eliminated.
176		3	Financial statements are prepared according to generally accepted accounting principles.
177		2	Financial records are kept using the double-entry system.
178		2	The accrual method is always used for management reports.
179		3	Personal and business expenses are never commingled.
180		2	Adequate records are kept for IRS requirements.
181		1	Payments on account are matched to invoices.
182		1	Allowance for doubtful accounts is reasonable.
183		2	Credits to accounts are properly approved.

Protection

Item	Score	Weight	Power Tool
184		3	Liability insurance is adequate to protect equity.
185		3	Insurance is adequate to prevent personal liability.
186		2	Management is aware of insurance coverage.
187		2	Coverage has been removed from retired assets.
188		2	Limits of coverage are reviewed annually.
189		2	Competitive bids on insurance are obtained.
190		1	Health insurance coverage is competitive.
191		1	Key person life insurance coverage is in place.
192		1	Deductible limits are at the most cost-effective levels.
193		2	Workers' compensation claims are monitored.
194		2	Claims are processed quickly.
195		2	Injured workers are encouraged to return to work ASAP.
196		1	Minor accidents are settled with a liability release.
197		2	Inventories are physically protected from damage or theft.
198		3	Security over fixed assets is adequate.
199		3	Legal counsel is competent and independent.

Item	Score	Weight	Power Tool
200		3	Legal counsel is consulted on all legal issues.
201		3	A competent tax preparer prepares the tax return.
202		3	Correspondence from governmental agencies is handled immediately.
203		3	All tax payments are made on time.
204		2	The company fosters a positive working relationship with its bank.
205		2	The bank is kept informed of the company's operations.
206		3	The company complies with all terms of its loan agreements.
207		2	Banking, legal and CPA relationships are changed only after careful consideration.
208		3	Management seeks and heeds professional advice in all technical disciplines.
209		2	New employee references are checked.
210		3	Dishonesty of any kind is not tolerated.
211		2	An effective safety program is followed.
212		2	The company complies with all governmental safety policies.
213		3	Hazardous working conditions are not tolerated.
214		2	Computer file backup is performed daily.
215		1	Computer backup is stored off-site.
216		1	An alternate source for data processing is available.
217		2	Data files are password protected.

Item	Score	Weight	Power Tool
218		2	Computer programs are documented, copied, and stored off-site.
219		3	Personnel policies are written.
220		3	Personnel policies are consistently administered.
221		3	One person coordinates personnel policy administration.
222		3	Policies address progressive discipline, discrimination and harassment.
223		2	All personnel complaints are investigated quickly and completely.
224		2	Everyone's work is subject to review and approval.
225		3	All credit is preapproved and routinely reviewed.
226		2	Past due accounts are monitored weekly.
227		3	Collection procedures are consistent, insistent, and persistent.
228		2	Legal counsel is used to send dunning letters.
229		1	Collection agencies are used when appropriate.
230		3	All leasing arrangements are reviewed by legal counsel.
231		2	Leases are evaluated for cost-effectiveness.
232		1	Excess funds are in short-term, interest-bearing investments.
233		2	Investments are made only with licensed, reputable brokers.

Item	Score	Weight	Power Tool
234		2	Maturities, yields, and principal balances of investments are carefully monitored.
235		2	Employees are cross trained to perform multiple jobs.
236		2	Workers are employees unless they can substantiate independent contractor status.
237		2	Computer programmer references are checked before the programmer is given access to computer programs.
238		1	Routine equipment maintenance is performed routinely.
239		2	The company complies with all legal notification requirements.

Production

Item	Score	Weight	Power Tool
240		2	The employees understand the company's organization.
241		2	Employees are taught how their tasks help the company to achieve its objectives.
242		3	Employees benefit from the company achieving its objectives.
243		3	Authority is delegated with responsibility.
244		2	All ideas for improvement are entertained.
245		3	Everyone is treated with dignity.
246		2	Employees are given feedback on all ideas.

Item	Score	Weight	Power Tool
247		2	Employees receive verbal and monetary rewards for input.
248		3	Performance evaluations are held regularly.
249		3	Poor performance is constructively criticized.
250		2	Consistently poor performance is penalized.
251		3	Quality performance is rewarded.
252		3	People are considered the company's most valuable resource.
253		2	Personnel problems are resolved as they arise.
254		2	Employees are trained in problem resolution.
255		2	Performance expectations are communicated to the employees.
256		2	All employees participate in ongoing training programs.
257		2	Productivity gains do not cause termination of good workers.
258		3	All managers are responsible for productivity.
259		2	The company is neat, clean, and orderly.
260		3	Redundancies are eliminated by handling a transaction the fewest times possible.
261		2	Employees are provided with the tools they need to do the job.
262		2	Management style fosters creativity by encouraging employees to ask "Is there a better way?"

Item	Score	Weight	Power Tool
263		2	The company rejects perfection in favor of action.
264		3	A logical flow of activities is defined and communicated to employees.
265		2	Activities are standardized.
266		3	The transfer of responsibility is standardized and understood by all parties.
267		3	Immediate action is taken to correct product flaws.
268		2	Records are kept of product returns and quality problems.
269		2	Products are engineered for ease in manufacture.
270		2	Monotonous tasks are periodically reassigned or distributed to several employees.
271		1	Work areas are ergonomically designed.
272		3	Management and employees understand it is cheaper to do the job right the first time.
273		2	Customers are given realistic delivery dates.
274		2	Delays are communicated to customers.
275		3	Production scheduling allows management to determine the status of each job in progress.